Communication, technology and the development of people

Investment in Third World development so far has failed to deal adequately with its social dimension – the development of people, communities and institutions. This book explores reasons for this persistent difficulty, and outlines solutions that new perceptions of the communication process in development and the role of digital utilities offer.

Bernard Woods shows how the root cause lies in the reductionism of Western education systems, the confines of the structures in which governments and doner agencies are now organized, and the development approaches that follow from them. By building a new conventional framework which links the potential of the information revolution and the communication sector with the social prerequisites of sustainable development, he offers a new way forward. The basis of this is new interactive technology systems which constitute a new form of public utility, and will, for the first time, provide a medium of immense potential through which to invest in the development of people. This will introduce new understandings of the communication sector in development; it will transform traditional approaches to education, health and government advisory services, and provide a basis for drawing the resources of the information industry into development.

The book describes the new paradigm for development that the combination of these advances introduces, outlines new opportunities that a major paradigm shift will open up, and the new hope that this offers for the future.

For fifteen years **Bernard Woods** held specialist positions in the World Bank, with an overview of World Bank assistance in the rural sector worldwide. For a decade he has sought causes of the apparent inability of conventional development approaches to deal adequately with the human/institutional dimension of sustainable development. He became involved with the latest advances in the social applications of new informatics systems and, in 1991, left the World Bank to work full time in this new field and to raise awareness internationally of the new conceptual and physical solutions these advances introduce.

Communication, technology and the development of people

Bernard Woods

With a Foreword by
John Sculley, Chairman and CEO,
Apple Computer, Inc

London and New York

First published 1993　# 26012715
by Routledge
11 New Fetter Lane, London EC4P 4EE

Simultaneously published in the USA and Canada
by Routledge
a division of Routledge, Chapman and Hall Inc.
29 West 35th Street, New York, NY 10001

© 1993 Bernard Woods

Typeset by LaserScript Limited, Mitcham, Surrey
Printed and bound in Great Britain by
Biddles Ltd, Guildford and King's Lynn

British Library Cataloguing in Publication Data

A catalogue record for this book is available from the British Library.

Library of Congress Cataloging in Publication Data

Woods, Bernard, 1939–
　Communication, technology, and the development of people/
　Bernard Woods.
　　p.　cm.
　Includes bibliographical references and index.
　ISBN 0–415–08775–9. – ISBN 0–415–08776–7 (pbk.)
　　1. Communication – Technological innovations　2. Communication –
Social aspects.　I. Title.
P96.T42W66　1993
302.2–dc20　　　　　　　　　　　　　　　　　　　92-20283
　　　　　　　　　　　　　　　　　　　　　　　　　　　CIP

Contents

Figures

Tables

Preface

> It is clear that the economic and social strategies that we have adopted have led us into a morass from which, it seems, there is no escape. We can get out, but [to do so] we need to reexamine the strategies that we have followed.
>
> (Julius Nyerere, 1981)

Much has been achieved in third world development in the decade since President Nyerere of Tanzania made this assessment, but small advances in one field seem to be negated by growing problems in others. New investment may have brought us closer to the brink of the morass, but has not established a basis for escaping from it.

Success in development to date has been partial. Many technical, physical, economic and financial objectives have been achieved, but solutions for human and social objectives, and for alleviating widespread poverty and debt, remain elusive. This book examines a fundamental and pervasive problem underlying the persistency and consistency of this experience, and describes solutions that will introduce a new era in development.

The evidence presented here outlines the nature of the difficulty. It shows how the problem is a product of conventional perceptions of 'development'; how new digital technology systems can help in our understanding of the nature of that problem and can also provide a new tool of enormous potential for addressing the development of people and the neglected social dimension of development. It shows that serious questioning of conventional systems and approaches is needed and indicates what this can make possible.

The author spent twelve years in two countries in Africa working in agriculture, rural development and tertiary education, then fifteen years working from the World Bank in Washington in third world countries worldwide. For ten of the latter, he had an overview of all the World Bank's lending for agriculture and rural development. He also had a view of lending for education, and of attention given to the training and institutional aspects of projects in other sectors too. From 1987 to 1990 he occupied the World Bank's Senior Specialist position in Development Communication.

Much of the experience quoted in the book reflects the author's background. Readers will be able to draw parallels from their own experience. The book touches on a very broad range of topics. Treatment of each one is inevitably brief in the interests of an easily readable volume for a wide readership. The book's focus is on the sum of (a) the common lessons from development experience across sectors and (b) where this, together with the social applications of interactive technologies and new perceptions of the communication process in development, can lead us in the future.

Foreword

We are on a verge of a transition from one world economic order to another – a fundamental shift that has the potential for bringing about one of the most exciting periods in human history. For most of this century, the industrialized countries succeeded by taking natural resources out of the ground – oil, crops and coal – adding manufacturing know-how to those resources and turning them into products. Then they developed services around these new products.

In a very short time we have seen a dramatic change in that economic system. Today we are no longer in the Industrial Age. We are in an information-intensive, global-dynamic economy. The resources are no longer just those that come out of the ground. The resources today come out of our minds. They are ideas and information.

This trend has huge implications in terms of the kinds of jobs that will be available for people around the world, and will have an enormous impact on the role of information technology in the developing world. The successful nations will be those that realize that the high-performance work organization will quickly replace the low-skilled, low-wage, industrial-based organizations of the past. The successful communities will be those that mobilize and manage their own natural and human resources.

A high-performance work organization is one that moves information swiftly and easily through its organization for decision and action. It is one that recognizes that information is the currency of modern life, and understands that the value a nation's workforce adds to the world economy is measured by the skills of that workforce. Therefore, high-performance work hinges on the quality of the skills of the workforce, and on how adept a workforce is at problem solving, identifying issues and communicating.

Of course, information technology can play a critical role in both the development and the constant upgrading of worker skills. But what is needed for this to happen is a fundamental shift in the way the world thinks about communication, learning and work, and the larger societal context in which those three exist.

It is important to realize that technology – particularly in the context of education – is no 'silver bullet'. It can help in engaging a student's interest in a subject, but it must be placed in a complete system that combines well-prepared teachers with integrated social services. Only when the complete system is designed that supports the whole student – throughout a lifetime of learning – will the full power of technology be realized.

As Bernard Woods argues, in order for the high-performance work organization to become more pervasive, we need to revisit some of the underlying principles that the education system has depended on during most of this century.

In the 1920s, Henry Ford set up mass production at the Ford Motor Company and industrial engineer Frederick Taylor defined work in a way that would make mass production efficient. The concept was relatively simple. Taylorism broke down work into the simplest possible tasks so that workers at the lowest levels of the hierarchy were expected to have no particular skills or knowledge. Tasks became so simple that almost anyone could perform them.

A series of managers or supervisors were above that individual, and each level would check the work of the level below. Both Ford and Taylor believed it was best to separate work into that which required 'thinking' and that which required 'doing'. So people working on the mass production manufacturing line were not expected to think. Their jobs were to perform repetitive tasks.

Separately, organizations would have a staff to do all of the thinking, analysis, planning, forecasting and budgeting.

These parallel – line and staff – organizations have been the structure of our industrial economy, and have provided the strength for mass producers around the world. Today, however, front-line workers are expected to make decisions regarding quality control, equipment maintenance and production scheduling.

In less developed countries, farmers and their families make up most of the front-line workers. More and more, they are faced with profound changes as a consequence of soil and forest degradation, market and currency fluctuations, water shortages and the need for off-farm employment. They, too, will need new perspectives, new skills and new work practices to cope with the rapidly changing nature of the world's work. At the most basic level, these communities will need to be empowered to handle these changes.

Empowerment is often seen as something one can 'do' to another person. This is not so. People are empowered by an environment that gives them the freedom to express themselves. Leadership is about creating such an environment that enables individuals to develop their potential to the fullest, and then encourages them to build on those skills and abilities for the future.

For the developed and the developing world alike, we cannot expect to succeed in the twenty-first century by merely extending the philosophies of the nineteenth century. Rather, we need to fundamentally rethink many of the principles and approaches that have guided our decision making for most of this century. This is at the heart of Bernard Woods' thesis.

Based on his extensive experiences with the World Bank, and as an expert in the area of communication and behaviour change in the developing world, he observes that the most successful development programmes are those that inspire individuals and organizations to develop their own systems and solutions to meet their own unique needs.

He gives examples of 'customized' development programmes that take full advantage of existing knowledge systems instead of superimposing systems that may have worked elsewhere but are inappropriate for a specific community.

At a more practical level, Woods offers an insightful discussion on how the lack of a global communication infrastructure will be a major obstacle in a community's ability to come 'into sync' with the rest of the world. Not only does he provide ample evidence of how a digital utility system, like a national information freeway, will have its obvious beneficiaries – libraries and educational institutions – he also gives examples of how other institutions, namely the health care system, will benefit from such a systematic change.

So, with the enlarged capacity of network technology that allows the transmission of audio and video signals, doctors will be able to 'visit' patients in remote locations. In addition, we will soon have the capability to put medical images on the network and have physicians in various clinics view them simultaneously.

But before this vision can become a reality, Woods calls for basic, institutional change. And rightly so. Not only do the existing institutions need to re-evaluate how they've done things in the past, but the leadership in these institutions must be willing – where appropriate – to let go of the tired old practices and procedures that may have worked before, but are entirely incompatible with an information economy.

In this new world of work, individuals will be increasingly asked to pour a part of themselves into the success of their communities. Individuals will also be asked for a greater commitment than in the days when they were simply a cog in the wheel of a systematized institution. In return, people should gain an experience that sharpens their instincts, teaches them the newest lessons, shows them how to become self-engaged in their work, and gives them new ways of looking at the world.

This does not mean open-ended loyalty. While they are in a community, people have to buy into the vision that guides it. Unlike any other time in history, the availability and accessibility of information is making it possible for individuals to have a clear understanding of a community's vision and what they must do to make it a reality.

It is refreshing to hear people like Bernard Woods talk about 'the development of the capacity of people, communities, and institutions.' This philosophy has always been at the root of progress, and must continue to be at the centre of every development effort, particularly those that focus on the introduction and adoption of information technology. As Woods points out, it is not the communications, computing or information processing technology that represent the value of an organization. It is its people.

Back in the mid-1980s, the General Secretary of the Communist Party of the former Soviet Union, Mikhail Gorbachev, selected me to serve on the board of the International Foundation for the Survival and Development of Humanity. This is an East–West cooperative effort on human rights, education, arms reduction, energy and the environment. In the course of our meetings and events, I learned an enormous amount about how the appropriate use of information technology can empower entire communities in parts of the world where there is virtually no infrastructure on which to build the future. But as the former Soviet premier told me on several occasions, the greatest challenge in any restructuring effort is knowing where to start. I am optimistic that the proposals for change that Bernard Woods carefully outlines in his book will give more people in more locations a place to begin.

John Sculley
Chairman and CEO
Apple Computer, Inc

Acknowledgements

This book would not have come about without the support and encouragement from my wife and family; their many patient hours at the computer and their inputs, and those of many friends and colleagues, to making a complex subject readable and comprehensible. Instrumental too in making the book possible is Jack Taub.

My thanks and appreciation are also due to Hillary Perraton for his thoughtful reviews of successive drafts, and to Bobby Srinivasan for his assistance with my education in new technology and with introductions in various parts of the world. A special word of acknowledgement is also due to Dr Kurt Hecht. He first showed me that the identities of the conventional disciplines and 'sectors' in which development investment has been packaged may differ from those given them by current traditions.

Chapter 1

The revolution

Perhaps the most fundamental implication of information is a perception. Although information is a part of the environment and an essential element of development, a consciousness and understanding of it is only just beginning.[1]

DEVELOPMENT EXPERIENCE

The past forty years have seen countries evolve from imperialism and colonialism to independent states; from capitalism to socialism and communism, and back again. These years have seen extraordinary progress in the development of new nations' physical infrastructure, industry and trade; increases in their levels of education, health, mortality, and income; movement of large numbers of people from subsistence to paid employment; migration from rural to urban areas, and much more. At the same time, advances in knowledge and technology have broadened the scope of development and changed priorities for new investment. Governments' successive national plans and the investment policies of major donor agencies over these years reflect both the prevailing conventional wisdom for development of the times, and member countries' changing priorities. They also record areas of persistent difficulty. The essence of the guiding rationale for development was the following.

'Westernization' was a primary driving force for investment in third world development until the 1950s. With countries' independence, this emphasis changed to 'modernization'. To be 'modern', it was thought, would cure the poverty of third world people. Investment in the 1950s focused on strengthening basic infrastructure – transportation systems, ports, electricity and water supplies, and on supporting industrial development and commercial agriculture through plantation crops, to obtain foreign exchange. This was needed to establish a sound basis for subsequent economic expansion.

In the 1960s, priority moved to increasing the productivity of large rural populations. The difficulties of reaching all of these people and of changing their commitment to their established ways were well known, but it was believed that if the more prominent among rural communities would adopt new methods, others would follow. The benefits would trickle down and eventually spread to whole societies. New investment concentrated on rural infrastructure, agricultural research, irrigation systems, rural access roads, water supplies, and production of cash crops and livestock for international markets. Better educated people were needed to run the expanding economies, and education was associated with quicker adoption of innovation. Lending for education by the World Bank began in 1963.

By the end of the decade, it was clear that these emphases alone were insufficient. More integrated approaches to rural sector development were needed. So the 1970s saw new attention to subsistence farming; big investment in most developing countries in agricultural and other advisory services, farm inputs, markets, agricultural credit, village access roads, and land conservation in attempts to reach, benefit, and mobilize massive populations of poor people. Investment in education expanded, and greater attention was paid to people's health. Robert McNamara's speech to the Board of Governors of the World Bank in Nairobi in 1973 drew attention to the need to 'reach the bottom 40 per cent of the population' in third world countries, who, it seemed, had largely failed to benefit from development approaches until then.[2]

By the end of the 1970s, much had been achieved, but there was growing evidence of (a) the continuing shortfalls of those programmes and approaches for reaching the majority of the intended beneficiaries, and (b) a general failure to achieve widespread sustainability in all but a few government programmes. The succession of economic 'take-offs' that modernization theory had predicted had generally failed to occur – with a few important exceptions such as Taiwan and South Korea. It seemed that Adam Smith's arm was not long enough for his 'hidden hand' of market forces to reach the poorer of the poor.[3] More money for development did not seem to be the answer. In addition, though much attention had been given to economic sustainability until then, more and more evidence had accumulated indicating that ecological sustainability locally, nationally, and internationally posed a greater problem for the world than economic sustainability alone. A concern growing among observers and practitioners alike was that materialism and sustainability seemed fundamentally irreconcilable.

The 1980s saw increasing disillusionment with the conventional approaches. It saw a casting about for solutions in 'basic needs'; 'institutional development', 'women's development', 'food security', 'structural adjustment', and belated attention was paid to previously unheeded warnings on growing debt, population, water shortage, unemployment, and environmental degradation. The omission of these ingredients of development from earlier approaches suggested inadequacies in the underlying rationale of those approaches.

At the same time, a large body of experience had built up demonstrating success in community-based development. With all but a few exceptions, however, this success was in many small, mostly non-government programmes. All these paid great attention to human and social factors, and helped villagers to mobilize their own resources and to understand and draw upon the services available to them from government programmes and other sources. This success suggested that these programmes and the approaches they employed included ingredients that were missing from the strongly physical, technical, economic, and financial criteria on which most 'mainstream' investment for development by governments and donor agencies had concentrated and been justified by until then.

A DIFFERENT PERCEPTION

In 1988, summing up the conclusions of joint work on 'Rethinking Development' by the Indian Council of Social Sciences Research, the United Nations University, and the United Nations Asian and Pacific Development Centre, Professor S. C. Dube wrote:

> In respect of economic growth and technological change – or development generally – the third world has moved from euphoria to despair. During this period its dream world has been shattered. Its newly gained political independence has failed to usher in the promised era of prosperity. This has

caused anguish to the people whose revolution of rising expectations has turned to a nightmare of mounting frustrations. The modernizing elite has found itself in a chastened mood; its planning and development strategies have faltered and failed. With a trail of unrealized utopias behind it, development has lost its mystique. The collapse of the classical paradigm of development has urged serious rethinking as well as a search for alternatives.[4]

Planning and policy documents and economic literature commonly include such assertions as: 'It is undeniable that increasing GNP is the purpose of development, and will benefit the people.' This creed has been a guiding star leading development investment to its present point. Professor Dube argues that:

Development approaches can no longer take the narrow goal of economic growth as their primary objective. If human needs and the quality of life, more broadly conceived, are seen and approached as the real goals of change, this will establish a new development paradigm.

Rural investment to achieve the Green Revolution in India has made the country an exporter of rice and wheat. This is an extraordinary accomplishment. At the same time, however, more than 500 million people remain illiterate or semi-literate in India – more than the entire population of Africa – and the numbers in absolute poverty have increased. The investments involved have achieved remarkable success in agricultural terms, but not in human/social terms. The same situation, on a smaller scale, pertains elsewhere.

The assertion that 'increasing GNP is the purpose of development' can, and needs to be, rewritten. It is *the development of people*, and of groups, communities and institutions that is the primary purpose of development – to permit them to achieve (among other things) lasting increases in GNP. This means more than increasing human productivity in a narrow economic sense. It includes their empowerment to understand and manage their own processes of change, as well as managing their physical and financial resources.

In 1986, Jamshid Gharajedaghi and Russel Ackoff wrote:

The most serious consequences of the lack of definition of development derive from mistaking *growth* for *development*.

Development has less to do with how much people have than with how much they do with whatever they have.[5]

A review of development literature across sectors in 1984, found this view expressed in many different ways, and from many different perspectives of development experience.[6] A decade earlier Manzoor Ahmed and Philip Coombs, in their book *Education for Rural Development* explored this subject in detail.[7] About the same time, Mahbul al Haq, a distinguished economist from Pakistan, wrote in his book *The Poverty Curtain*:

Development styles should be such as to build development around people rather than people round development.

Earlier still, in 1969, an evaluation of agricultural assistance by the United States Agency for International Development (USAID) in Latin American countries in the 1960s came to a similar conclusion. An extensive literature now advocates the social priorities of development, but an adequate conceptual and practical basis for achieving that objective does not yet exist.

Third world countries are not alone in their difficulties. The following is taken from a speech by Bill Clinton, Governor of Arkansas, in 1991:

Ironically, at the very moment of history that American ideas (of democracy) are being embraced elsewhere, our own position is being weakened because of deficiencies in human capital. People may say ten or twenty years from now: 'The United States was the greatest democracy, the greatest military power, the greatest economic power in history, but by the end of the twentieth century it went into decline because Americans could not figure out how to fulfill their most basic need: how to raise and educate their children.'

The economies and societies of other western countries are similarly at risk.

The fact that the development of people, and not GNP, is the primary objective of development, is more than a semantic difference. It introduces a different basis for action. A basis for the different paradigm for development that Dube and many others have concluded must exist. (Paradigms are discussed in detail in Chapter 6.)

In pursuit of the physical, technical, and economic priorities of earlier decades, investment dealt with the development needs of roads, railways, crops, livestock, forests, dams, schools, hospitals, water and power supplies, sewage systems, and other government services. The means for achieving these objectives are in place. Macro-economic planning has been concerned with allocating resources among these physical options. All are needed! All are parts of 'development'. A stated objective of most of this investment was 'to benefit the people', but, of all the funds invested to achieve those physical objectives, only a tiny fraction has been spent on the inputs needed to develop the capacity of people. The means for achieving this on a large scale are still missing.

A DIFFERENT PARADIGM

A paradigm is called for in which both the physical *and* the social objectives of development can be addressed equally. Few would dispute this. But major changes in paradigm do not come about readily. New paradigms are founded on changes in concepts; they introduce new frameworks of thinking. Such changes confront the prevailing orthodoxy. Entrenched thinking and existing organizational structures and approaches delay acceptance of new concepts, however 'right' those changes may be. (In Europe, it took a hundred years for general acceptance that the world is round!)

Intellectual paradigms, on their own, change slowly. Major changes in paradigm come about much more quickly when new concepts are accompanied by new technology that make different approaches and solutions possible. We are at that rare point in history now.

Growing realization and acceptance that approaches to date have been fundamentally inadequate in dealing with the human/social dimension of development coincides with the appearance of a new technology which has enormous and unique potential for helping to address this very problem.

Professor Harry Johnson said:

> New ideas win a public and professional hearing not on their scientific merits, but on whether or not they promise a solution to important questions that the established orthodoxy has proved itself incapable of solving.

Exactly that situation exists now – as later chapters will show.

Human development functions and the roles of different communication media

An economic value has been given to investment in formal education. Education systems have had a place in economic planning. An equivalent economic value has not been given to the development of information and communication systems to address the learning needs of adults – or, for example, those of the 98 per cent of children in Africa and China who do not complete formal schooling. Communication systems have not had an equivalent place in macro-economic planning over the past 40 years, or in countries' investment programmes.

We can assess the potential of different communication channels for addressing the essential human and institutional development *functions* on which growth and sustainability depend. These functions, plus entertainment, are shown on one axis of Table 1.1 Different communication media are shown on the other. The Table indicates the *relative potential* of the different media for assisting with each essential function.

Implications of the analysis in Table 1.1 include the following:

1   Informatics systems, combining the communication capability of telephony and broadcasting, and the interactivity, processing, and multi-media capability of the computer, introduce new tools with enormous potential for assisting a wide range of critical human and institutional functions for development.

2   The breadth of applications of these technologies now enables us to invest in informatics and other communication systems specifically for addressing human and institutional development – as an objective of development in their own right, rather than as a subsidiary input in the achievement of physical, 'production' objectives (e.g. roads, irrigations, crops, power supplies.)

3   Table 1.1 indicates the inadequacy of the tools that have been available with which to address the whole human, institutional dimension of development prior to the arrival of the means for integrating electronic communication media.

Virtually every government is now faced with unmanageable costs and unsatisfactory performance of traditional education, health, advisory, and penal services. These would constitute a crisis

Table 1.1 Comparative potential of different communication media

Functions	Communication media							
	Press	Books	Radio	TV	Phone	Phone+	Computers	Informatics
Topical information	XXX		XX	XXX	XX	XX	X	XX
Formal education	X	XX	X	X	X	XX	XX	XXX
2-way communication			X		XXX	XXX	X	XXX
Interactive learning		X			X	XX	XX	XXX
Skill development		X		X	X	XX	XX	XXX
Motivation	X	X	X	XX	XX	XX	X	XX
Entertainment	X	X	X	XXX		X	X	XXX
Group decisions	X		X	XX	X	XX	X	XXX
Data supply	X	XX				XX	XX	XXX
Data processing						X	XXX	XXX
Planning		X			XX	XX	XX	XXX
Design		X				X	XX	XXX
Financing					X	X	XX	XXX
Monitoring					X	XX	XX	XXX
Financial control		X			X	XX	XX	XXX

Notes:

1 'Phone' refers to traditional, voice only telephone services. 'Phone+' (also called 'telematics') is what becomes possible with teleconferencing, and with networks and data bases where telephony links remote computers to mainframe computers. 'Informatics' goes beyond telematics reorder by decentralizing substantial memory and processing power to local level, and linking the uses of the whole family of digital technologies.

2 Printed and broadcast media have potential in most of the functions other than those for which they are given a rating in the Table 1.1, but their relative potential in those functions is small.

3 One can argue over the relative potential of one communication medium over another. For example: is TV more entertaining than radio or books? what is their potential in supplying data? A medium able to communicate in sound, pictures, graphics and script has a greater potential in these fields than media able to communicate only with literate people. Broadcast media have the disadvantage that the information and entertainment they offer is sent at the convenience of the broadcaster not the viewer or listener. (Video recorders are being used increasingly to overcome this difficulty in relation to TV.) A medium able to provide information and interactive learning and entertainment materials on demand has greater potential than those that cannot.

without the exacerbating effects of growing populations, and the need to address 'new' priorities, such as increasing employment, protecting the environment, decentralizing the initiative for development, meeting the needs of minorities and people with disabilities, and other objectives for which approaches to date have not contained adequate solutions. All these now compete for governments' limited resources.

A new option for development and a basis for questioning the adequacy of the prevailing development paradigm are introduced by the combination of a new perception of the communication process in development for human capital formation, the advent of a new tool with immense potential for addressing this objective, and the opportunity this introduces for transferring some of the burden of public services to the private sector.

A CHOICE

Current praxis has equated with 'development' the sum of the activities of the existing government ministries and departments and those of industry, business and services. Governmental structures and budgetary allocations for their activities can be represented as slices of a cake (see Figure 1.1). 'New' priorities have now appeared, referred to above. They span rather than fit conveniently within any one of the traditional sectors. They have had little place in macro-economic planning and budgetary allocations until now.

Thus we have a choice:

(a) Do we re-cut the cake, reducing the slice for each traditional sector to release funds for the new components? or:
(b) Since we formally equated the sum of the activities of the conventional sectors with 'development' and now find that these equal only part of development, was there something fundamentally amiss with that earlier guiding thinking which has obscured a different option?

Governments and major donor agencies have chosen (a). Allocations to existing sectors have been reduced in order to provide funds for the new priorities within governments' same limited resources. But all sectors have not been treated equally. Typically, planners in governments and their counterparts in major donor agencies have given priority to 'productive' sectors at the expense of the social sectors.

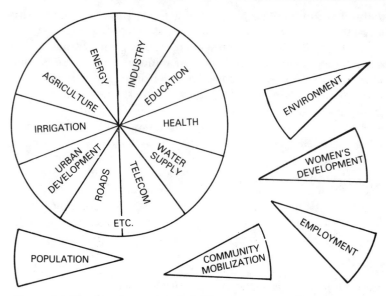

Figure 1.1 The development 'cake'. (The diagram does not attempt to show all government ministries.)

This has been a feature of 'structural adjustment' programmes in recent years. These have provided bridging funds to financially beleaguered governments. Their rationale has been as follows. Previous investments, based on the best available technical expertise in each sector, and with satisfactory economic rates of return, must have been 'right'. Their failure to perform as predicted must be due to market factors. Therefore, provide governments with more money to buy time for the expected results to materialize; simultaneously, change policies, institutional conditions, and incentive structures to correct market distortions, and all will be well.

There have been benefits from these programmes. But, when baking a cake, more heat cannot compensate for essential, missing ingredients. The essential human/social ingredients have been missing from the conventional recipe for development. More money is not the answer. Structural adjustment programmes have provided more money without introducing the solutions needed – and so have increased countries' debt.

In 1989, a group of African governments publicly challenged 'structural adjustment' on the grounds that such programmes did not attend to the social dimension of development, nor to what they called 'the real needs of Africa'. But their challenge was in terms of the relative allocations within existing sectors and approaches. This was easily disputed by conventional economic dogma. We can now establish a conceptual framework within which the African governments' case can be 'heard', and in which that case can be shown to be indisputable. Option (a), as offered above, is not an adequate solution. This suggests that we need to look to option (b). If we do so, exciting possibilities and new solutions emerge.

NEW CONCEPTS AND NEW TOOLS.

The Information Revolution is more than the technology itself. Integrated digital technologies (informatics) introduces a single tool with which to address a broad range of human and institutional development functions (as shown in Table 1.1). This will help us to see the identity of the whole human/social dimension of development differently. It calls for allocation of resources to realize the potential of the technology and concepts. These advances apply across all traditional 'sectors', and raise fundamental questions.

We can re-draw Figure 1.1, as shown in Figure 1.2, to reflect:

(a) the central objective of learning for developing people and institutions for their self-sustaining development, and
(b) the roles of communication (and hence communication systems) for achieving learning, management and governance in all sectors.

A new focus on communication systems and the potential of digital technology for addressing the human and institutional functions listed in Table 1.1, will open up a new chapter in development. This will:

(a) benefit all present sectors – as well as provide the means for addressing the human dimension of fields of 'new' priority;
(b) draw telecommunication and informatics from the periphery of investment to become a central tool for development in the future;
(c) Draw the private sector into the delivery of public services for the first time on a large scale (which is sensational for governments everywhere).

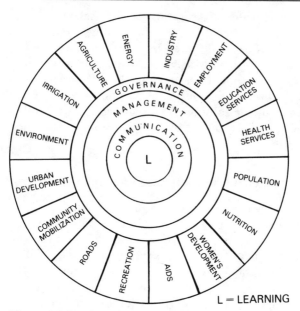

Figure 1.2 An alternative development 'cake'.

(d) Draw into the information marketplace the large proportion of the world's population that has been excluded from that marketplace until now;

(e) Provide new investment opportunities for the development funding agencies, and

(f) Carry development beyond the confines of current orthodoxy.

In this new framework of thinking, the roles of information and communication systems in development (all communication systems – not just digital technologies) will no longer be regarded as being peripherals in the achievement of conventional physical goals. Communication systems have a place in 'development' and in macro-economic planning in their own right for the *development of people.* An understanding of this will change perceptions of what 'development' is. It will open up a whole realm of new solutions and opportunities. It can introduce a revolution in thinking within which to approach the critical and neglected human dimension of development.

CONCLUSION

The central principles underlying the case this book presents can be summarized in the following way.

1   The primary objective of 'development' is to increase the capacity of people, communities, and institutions. This requires investment in communication systems in order to achieve the information transfer, learning, and behaviour change needed for that development, plus the planning, management, and governance needed to direct and sustain all development activities. The essential communication process this involves has so far not been a central part of guiding thinking for 'development'.

2   Most of the guiding thinking for macro-economic planning and development investment until now has equated 'human resource development' and 'human capital formation' narrowly with investment in traditional approaches to basic education and basic health. 'Institutional development' and 'women's development' have been added more recently to the rubric for the social dimension of development. Investment to achieve those objectives (in the name of 'human resource development') has fallen far short of what has been needed to address the full range of the essential human and institutional development functions on which self-sustaining development depends.

3   Approaches to communication, and the communication systems in place until now, have been inadequate to reach and influence whole populations – or to achieve the information transfer and learning in all fields needed for self-sustaining development.

4   It is now possible to explain why the obvious need to develop people and institutions in order to achieve development objectives has not been central to development investment to date.

5   Digital technologies are merging old distinctions between broadcasting, telephony, printing, and computing. Their interactive capacity, and their ability to communicate on demand in sound, pictures and graphics, as well as in script and numbers, introduces a communication medium of immense potential for a wide range of human development functions. Integrated digital technology systems, linking these technologies provide a new entity in which to invest specifically for developing people and institutions. (This supplements but does not replace existing communication systems.)

6   New perceptions of the roles of information and learning, and of communication systems in development, will enable

'development' to move beyond the confines of current approaches.

The following chapters examine the experience and new advances that support the case outlined above.

Chapter 2 examines conventional approaches to communication and learning for development to date and the inherent limitations of approaches based on using narrowly trained people as the embodiment of knowledge and primary medium of communication. It describes the communication 'sector', new approaches that interactive technologies and new perceptions of the communication process in development can open up, and joint action needed by governments and the information industry to develop this sector.

Chapter 3 outlines a fundamental, underlying cause of the neglect until now of the development of people, and of the communication process and communication systems needed for doing so.

Chapter 4 describes the nature of new software delivery systems and the new form of public utility they constitute for the future, and working examples which demonstrate the potential of the social applications and public use of this new phenomenon.

Chapter 5 explores challenging (and some surprising) implications and applications that follow from a re-assessment of traditional disciplines and sectors in the light of new, cross-sectoral approaches to the communication process and the human/institutional dimension of development.

Chapter 6 discusses the new paradigm created by the combination of the above and the basis which this provides for moving beyond the confines of current orthodoxy. It shows how an understanding of the nature of the major paradigm shift for development which is now before us can accelerate the achievement of the new paradigm – and the array of opportunities that lie within it.

Chapter 2

Present approaches for communication, learning and behaviour change

I

> If development is not growth, not resources, not wealth alone –
> what is it? I think it is, above all, learning. The learning needed
> by individuals, communities, and nation states to prepare
> themselves to live in the future.[1]

Development is about increasing the capacity of individuals,
families, communities, local authorities, private organizations,
central governments and nations to plan and manage their own
resources and affairs. Therefore it is also about putting in place the
systems to create the knowledge, skills, attitudes, policies and
institutions for doing so, and about developing people's capability
to use and maintain those systems.

Success has been achieved worldwide in building roads, dams,
railways, telephone systems, industries, schools, hospitals, research
stations, government services, and much else. Far less success has
been achieved in developing the communication, learning and
management processes needed to create the capacity of people,
and of communities and institutions, to benefit from and sustain
those advances. The familiar organizations of governments –
ministries of transport, education, agriculture, irrigation, health,
and so on – have been set up and strengthened to do the former.
They have each tried, but have not been adequately equipped, to
do the latter.

Governments everywhere are now faced with 'new' priorities on
a massive scale: environmental degradation; unemployment;
population growth; malnutrition; needs for women's
development; decentralization of governance; community

mobilization; and water and energy conservation. Government agencies need to be able to communicate, change attitudes, create new understandings and change behaviour in all of these fields. The traditional government ministries (and their equivalents in donor agencies) have not had the necessary skills, mandates or orientation to cope with these topics.

In looking closely at third world development experience, one finds that success in government-led development has been achieved among those people, and in those fields of activity, in which governments and other development workers have been able to communicate effectively. Conversely, one finds common features across 'sectors', countries and continents in:

(a) The inability of the governmental systems in place for development to communicate adequately with all segments of the groups and communities they are attempting to assist;

(b) The content of most development communication being strongly confined to the technical fields of the organizations currently in place to achieve development;

(c) The limited use that has been made of mass communication media in reaching and influencing the majority of urban and rural populations, and the fact that most governments and donor agencies have lacked the guiding policies needed for doing so;

(d) The fact that the emphasis placed on sending information has not been matched by attention to how that information is received and interpreted or to the decision making processes that that information is intended to influence.

Thus, adequate communication with the majority of countries' urban and rural populations has been, and continues to be, a pervasive problem worldwide. The means to achieve the necessary communication and behaviour change are not yet in place.

Something has obstructed, and continues to obstruct, the obvious need to develop the abilities of people for their own self-sustaining development.

Better universal understanding is required of both the nature of the problem and the new remedies that are at hand. We first need to examine the nature of the problem, then to consider the role of mass communication systems in providing solutions, and the implications and future roles of digital technologies with their unique ability to interact with users on demand and to communicate in sound, pictures and graphics as well as in script and numbers.

FRAGMENTATION OF THE COMMUNICATION PROCESS

A key feature of the problem is that conventional approaches to development have fragmented the communication process and the development and use of mass communication media among the various technical agencies in which governments and donor agencies are organized.

In colonial days in most of the less developed countries, the field services of government ministries and departments were established primarily for regulatory and administrative purposes for crops, livestock production and health, grazing control, plant protection, soil conservation, forestry, health, water use, and others. Only relatively recently – within the last 35 years – have their roles changed to predominantly advisory and educational functions. This accompanied the increasing emphasis in the 1960s and 70s on raising productivity of the rural masses and reaching 'the bottom 40 per cent of the population'. It called for communication in every technical field to change the beliefs, attitudes and behaviour of large, predominantly rural populations. Each of the various government agencies separately attempted to expand and reorient their field services to do so.

The need for communication was obvious to those responsible for progress in every technical field. Mass communication infrastructure was either not in place or its coverage was limited, so each government agency had to rely on people to be its primary medium of communication. Each agency employed more and more people, either as teachers or as field workers in their many field services, to transfer knowledge and change behaviour. More agencies have been established, each with its individual development objectives and projects, and promoted by competing donors. In one Asian country, the Ministry of Agriculture alone had sixteen different agencies, each with its own small army of field staff, all separately trying to communicate with farmers. The cost of this approach finally grounded the whole system. The system itself was the problem. Each agency had attempted to become its own communication channel.

People as a communication medium

At earlier stages of development, government agencies had to rely on people to be their primary medium of communication. All along, the limited number of trained staff that each ministry and department has been able to employ, train and manage has been the factor most limiting its ability to reach and influence its intended beneficiaries.

People have severe limitations as a communication medium. They are confined by what they know; their individual communication skills; their mobility; whom they like; who likes them; whom they meet; their age; their health; and cultural obstacles. (In Muslim countries, for instance, and in other cultures, males can have little direct communication with females outside their own families.)

Typically, most of the staff now employed in third world governments' parallel technical services are male (except among health, home economics and nutrition workers where the preponderance is generally female). Most of these staff have limited training in their technical fields and have limited mobility; many are poorly motivated. Their training and their jobs confine the content of their communication to their respective technical fields. Individually and collectively, they are unable to communicate the information and create the skills needed in the fields of 'new' priorities mentioned above.

No government anywhere can employ, update and manage enough staff in all of the different technical fields to supply the learning needed by whole populations. In fact, it would be hard to devise a more inefficient approach to communication and behaviour change than one which depends on the performance of many parallel field workers, individually attempting to reach and influence large numbers of rural or urban people. But this is the approach being followed in most third world countries.

The problems are more fundamental than numbers of teachers and field workers. Examples from education and agriculture illustrate the point.

Formal education

The primary, and often exclusive, medium for achieving learning in formal education systems has been teachers. Consequently, these systems are heavily confined by:

(a) The numbers of teachers that those systems can employ;
(b) The knowledge and communication capabilities of individual teachers;
(c) The degree of interaction that teachers can achieve with their students. (A recent study in the US public school system found an average interaction between teachers and children of two minutes per day. When one considers that most teachers interact mainly with a minority of children, the average interaction between the teachers and the majority of children is a matter of seconds per week!)

So that teachers can cope with prescribed teaching content and examination requirements, the universe of knowledge has to be reduced to manageable subsets – leading to the familiar subjects, curricula, timetables and examinations in which formal education has been organized.

In doing this, teaching content, time and place have been fixed, and student achievement has had to be the variable. We have all grown up with this system of formalized learning and with its inherent inability to accommodate the varying learning styles, rates and needs of the slower or more gifted learners and learners with widely disparate backgrounds. We have equated this approach with 'education'. We have lived with its shortcomings – in the absence of a viable alternative. The solutions needed in education worldwide, however, do not appear to lie in the traditional system. The system itself is the problem!

Various technologies and aids to learning have evolved: blackboards, textbooks, laboratories, calculators, films, radio, television and now computers. These technologies have almost invariably been used as add-ons to the conventional, teacher-centred system. There are exceptions. In the Radio Learning Programme in Kenya, for example, the children responded directly to instructions from teachers speaking over the radio. In other distance learning programmes, radio, television, printed and tape recorded materials are used in various combinations as the media of instruction. Students interact directly with instructional programmes – instead of the technology being used as teacher aids. The roles of the telephone and teleconferencing are expanding too. These demonstrate that different approaches to formal learning are possible, but they remain at the periphery of the mainstream of conventional approaches to education worldwide. They have not altered the traditional system.

In 1968, Robert McNamara said: 'It is important to emphasize that education, normally one of the largest employers, is one of the few industries which have not undergone a technological revolution.'[2] In 1983 the National Commission on Excellence in Education in the USA concluded:

> The raw materials needed to reform our education system were waiting to be mobilised through effective leadership. Almost a decade later, we have not achieved significant reform.

And:

> If an unfriendly power had attempted to impose on America the mediocre education system we have today, we might well have viewed it as an act of war.

Similar sentiments have been expressed on public platforms in most of the more economically advanced countries – and the same basic system had been imposed widely throughout the third world.

In 1992, Dr Richard L. Lesher, President of the United States Chamber of Commerce wrote:

> They say our schools are failing, but that is wrong. Our schools are as good as ever. The problem is that the world has changed. . . . Our educators are doing their best, but they are trying to serve 21st century students with boring 19th century methods – blackboards, chalk, pencils, and too often outdated textbooks.[3]

Mr McNamara's statement, twenty years ago, is still generally true today.

The Open University in the UK and replicas of this model currently being developed in eighteen other countries, with their extensive use first of radio and now of television, have introduced a technological revolution in the subset of education with which they deal. Computer-based learning is now being added. Student numbers have grown remarkably, but still this and other distance learning programmes affect only a small fraction of learners and the universe of learning.

Agriculture

Field workers (extension agents) have been used as the primary embodiment of knowledge and medium of communication in agricultural field services in the same way that teachers have in formal education. Their difficulties are even greater than those of teachers in that:

(a) They have to travel to meet their learners;
(b) Their learners are highly heterogeneous in their age, social standing, level of education and learning needs;
(c) In many cultures, custom has prevented extension agents from communicating directly with sizeable subsets of the farming community.

The problem is more than simply numbers of staff. The Director of an agricultural programme in Pakistan, when discussing agricultural advisory services on one occasion with the author, said:

You people in the West don't understand. In our country, knowledge has value. As an extension agent, I would not give my knowledge to you unless I could expect something in return. I wouldn't give my knowledge to that man over there because I know he cannot repay me. I wouldn't want even to be seen in the company of low class people. As for communicating with women [who do much of the agricultural work], our culture prevents me from speaking directly to them.

The author, returning to one African country in which he had worked twenty years previously, found that over 90 per cent of the agricultural recommendations had remained unchanged on topics regarded as key constraints to agricultural production. Agricultural extension agents had been walking or cycling around delivering the same messages for more than twenty years. Scientists had assessed and confirmed the correctness of the technical recommendations, but had not questioned the adequacy of the communication systems where the recommendations had not been adopted.

A study on one island in the Philippines showed that 40 per cent of farmers had never spoken to an extension agent – and did not believe that they had a right to do so. A study of the performance of a rural development project in one State in Nigeria found that only 3 per cent of farmers were contacted regularly by extension agents.

At the height of new investment in agricultural extension

services in the late 1970s, the government of one Asian country assembled data on the trained agricultural staff required for all of its current agricultural services and projects and for all of the new projects being planned. The government projected the increasing costs of those people as they all advanced up their salary scales. The figures showed that the total salary cost of all of the staff needed in all of the separately planned projects would be nearly double the amount provided for salaries in the next five year plan. (A similar exercise at the time would have produced much the same picture in many developing countries.) These data were presented at a meeting of the Secretary for Agriculture and the Director of the Central Planning Office. After absorbing the implications of the data, the Director of Planning said to the author: 'You World Bank, FAO, USAID and other donor agencies come to our country and tell us how to develop our agriculture. Now you tell us that we can't afford it.'

Like others have done, he was equating the development of agriculture with the existing extension system as the communication medium needed to do so. With a different perception, he would have said, 'You donor agencies are advocating a communication system for improving our agriculture which cannot be sustained countrywide, and therefore is inherently faulty.'

A study commissioned by USAID in 1975 carried out a detailed examination of 36 rural development projects sponsored by various institutions in 11 countries in Africa and Latin America. The work included 'an examination of the success of the knowledge transfer/acquisition process measured by major behaviour changes in production practices'. Performance was assessed in relation to various forms of extension services, methods, accountability and frequency of contact. Overall, traditional extension services – delivered by area-based agricultural experts dealing with individual farmers – were found to be the least effective mechanism for transmitting useful and used agricultural knowledge. (On the positive side, the work suggested that the accountability of extension workers to the local population contributed significantly to the effectiveness of extension work.)

Despite realities of this kind, governments and donors throughout the 1970s and early 80s continued to expand parallel government field services in every discipline. Each agency and department has tried to become its own communication channel, often funded separately by competing external donors, in the belief that face-to-face contact is essential for changing behaviour.

A great deal has been invested in the Training and Visit (T & V) system of agricultural extension. The system is based on regular, fortnightly training of field staff in selected technical messages and associated field practices. In theory, the staff pass on the information and skills to farmers and local 'contact farmers' at scheduled fortnightly visits at prearranged locations. The system has improved accountability, knowledge and morale in agricultural field services, and information flow between field staff and researchers. There have been increases in agricultural production, particularly in irrigated areas of very uniform agricultural conditions. But T & V is not an adequate solution.

The approach was devised to increase the efficiency of existing agricultural extension services. It did not question the validity of those services as a communication medium, nor the role of field extension staff in relation to other communication channels. Once the euphoria associated with large new investments in the agricultural services subsided, governments found themselves left with expanded field cadres in which large numbers of young staff are all moving up their salary scales without compensating loss from higher salary echelons. In Thailand, two extension/crop production projects alone added 8,700 staff to the Ministry of Agriculture. This increase in the cost of the services is continuing. It is accompanied by diminishing increases in agricultural production and persistent inadequacy in staff/farmer interaction.

There is a fundamental problem with the T & V approach. The delivery of prescribed messages according to a routine of occasional visits to farmers assumes:

(a) Homogeneity in farmers' needs;
(b) Individual rather than group decision making;
(c) Uniformity in the way that farmers receive and understand technical information;
(d) That farmers want, and so will accept, advice when it is convenient for the field staff to deliver it.

Studies of how farmers receive and interpret information, and of their decision making processes, indicate that the opposite to all four is generally the case. This is particularly true of sub-sistence farming.

The T & V approach has brought agricultural extension systems, based on large numbers of agricultural staff being the primary medium of communication with farmers, closer to the limits of their efficiency. It cannot overcome those limits because they are inherent in the conventional extension system. The problem is the system![4]

Research has shown that a great deal of change in practice among subsistence farmers depends on group decisions. This differs from western cultures and conditions of more advanced agriculture where individual decision making is the norm. Group decision making calls for different approaches to the communication required. Radio drama has a big advantage here. It can feed new ideas to communities and groups on a daily basis – often disguised within the drama. This can promote internal discussion and changes of perceptions within groups and communities which then lead to agreement to change accepted practices.

Different studies of the comparative cost of farmer contact by radio and by field extension workers have come up with figures for radio being between 30 and 3,000 times less expensive than field workers. Various forms of mass media have also shown their ability to reach women and deprived sections of communities and remote villages on a large scale and sustainable basis. No one can claim that radio (or any other mass communication medium) can substitute fully for face-to-face contact. But the very substantial relative cost of field workers should prompt the question: for what purposes are field extension workers needed that cannot be provided by more cost effective means of communication? Curiously, throughout the enormous investment in third world countries during the 1970s and 80s to expand governments' many field services, this question has not been seriously addressed at national planning levels.

MASS COMMUNICATION

Much research worldwide has concluded that each medium of communication has advantages over others for certain purposes and in specific situations. Hence, if governments are to develop the capacity of people and institutions, they need to be concerned with the best use of all communication media.

Shortcomings referred to above, resulting from attempts to achieve face-to-face contact as the primary medium of communication for development, do not mean that teachers and instructors are not needed, or that alternatives and supplements for human communication agents have not been tried. For the past fifteen years, the *Development Communication Report* [5] and the *Agricultural Information Development Bulletin* [6] have documented innovative uses of all kinds of communication media in support of government and NGO programmes in virtually every country in the world. Significantly, many of the most innovative and successful uses of mass communication have been in those 'newer' fields, such as population control and, more recently, AIDS, which lack large numbers of extension workers. They have drawn upon the expertise of the advertising industry and their 'social marketing' techniques.

Different initiatives have demonstrated the potential of every communication channel – broadcast, print, telephones, tape recorders, video, postal services, mobile information vans, puppetry and traditional communication systems. (The last includes traditional theatre, dance, story tellers and drums.) Yet, with a few exceptions, funding of these initiatives has been an add-on to conventional approaches by one field service of government or another to achieve an agricultural, livestock, immunization, water use, health or other objective.

All countries have developed their radio and television systems, their printing and telephone capabilities and their postal services. When doing so, however, few have integrated the use of such a capability with the day-to-day management of their advisory field services. Examples exist which demonstrate that this can be done. The Rural Radio Programme in Liberia shows how the use of radio can be integrated with field services. The programme established a decentralized production and broadcasting capability and created the institutional structures for the management of its use by a variety of the different field services.

A programme in Mali demonstrates the potential of rural newspapers in a multi-sectoral support role. A programme in Peru demonstrates how the telephone can be integrated with field advisory services. A programme in Kenya demonstrates how traditional communication systems can be strengthened on a national basis and at low cost through the training, organization and support of story tellers, theatre groups, choirs, dancers, puppeteers and drummers – all of whom have their roles as communication channels in their country's traditions.

Interesting examples can be found in every country in the world. But, with only a few exceptions, all are isolated programmes. They have been achieved in the absence of guiding national policies to direct the coordinated use of communication media. In the absence of such policies, many of these successes remain largely unknown and unreplicated.

Two-way communication

Most forms of print and broadcast media are one-way – with serious limitations as communication channels. Video is being used increasingly as a two-way medium. It is now widely used for assisting learning and for supporting decision making within communities. It has also been used successfully as a low cost medium for communication between rural communities and distant policy makers. The Proderith rural development programme in Mexico demonstrates this well, as does a rural banking project in India, and there are many other examples.

The superior two-way capability of the telephone for communicating and achieving behaviour change has been demonstrated by a variety of programmes in different countries. This medium has been seriously under-utilized in development to date. Advances in electronics are expanding the uses of telephones from voice alone to electronic mail, fax, access to data bases, teleconferencing and other applications. But telecommunication remains an expensive communication medium whose use is still largely confined to those able to pay a significant price to communicate with distant sources of information.

These examples, and a great many others around the world, all provide clues to the role and nature of information and the communication process in development. But governments and donor agencies still lack policies for a holistic approach to the development and use of each communication channel in its most effective role. Digital technologies are a recent arrival on the scene. By 1987, electronics became the world's fourth largest industry, with worldwide production of $US500 billion. All but a small fraction of the investment and technology, however, served the markets in business, industrial, and military applications. A significant proportion has also been devoted to developing entertainment applications. These technologies can now profoundly alter approaches to communication and learning and to the whole human/social dimension of development in the future. In 1991, John L. Clendinin, Chairman of Bell South, said:

> In large part, how well we incorporate technology into the education of our children will ultimately determine how competitive we remain in the global, technically driven economy.

The same can be said for the role of technology in the much larger lifelong learning process, and the role of that process in a rapidly changing world.

THE COMMUNICATION REVOLUTION

> A popular belief in academic circles has been that the only way to educate anyone is to arrange face-to-face encounters between the student and the teacher, so that 'two minds can rub against each other'. This was a charming conceit of the élite in the nineteenth century. It is an intolerably expensive fallacy in the twentieth century.[7]

The long awaited revolution in education of which Robert McNamara spoke in 1968 (referred to on page 20) is now at hand.

Informatics – meaning the combination of the communication capabilities of telecommunication; the processing power of computers; the memory capability of CD-ROM, optical disk and other storage technology; and the presentational capacity of multi-media (using sound, video, graphics, numbers and script) – now makes it possible to deliver instructional materials electronically to learners of all kinds, individually and on demand.

In formal education, the technology's ability for personal interaction allows 'customized' instruction. Teachers can allocate interactive learning material individually to every child (see Chapter 4). This allows students to learn at their own pace and in their own way, and to pursue their own interests and aptitudes in addition to completing required learning. Until now, formal learning for children has had to take place in classrooms during specified times. We can now change the time and place where formal learning can happen.

For the first time on a large scale, it is possible for instructional content and time to be made the variables, and for required student achievement to become the standard. Interactive technologies provide a tool with which to overcome the inherent problem of using teachers as the embodiment of knowledge and primary medium of communication with students. The problem has been the inherent limitations of traditional education systems. The technology can help to change those systems.

This advance does not do away with teachers. Instead, it releases teachers from the drudgery and inefficiency of personally having to teach basic literacy, numeracy, facts and concepts to every child. Experience is showing that children can acquire much basic knowledge faster from interactive computer learning, and accompanying peer instruction, than they can in traditional classroom settings. This allows teachers to spend more time managing the learning process, attending to the special learning needs of individuals, and on developing the social and spiritual understandings that have been so much a victim of rationalistic, modern western education.

Digital technologies which can provide an interactive learning source for one subset of learning – that which has traditionally been intended to take place in schools – can do so for others. Digital systems, together with the realization of the full potential of other communication media, can help to overcome the inherent problems of governments' traditional field advisory services in agriculture, health and all the other fields referred to above. Communities can use interactive instructional materials as and when they need them. Agricultural recommendations can be converted into digital form and stored locally in Community Information and Learning Centres. The same can be done with diagnostic materials for humans, livestock and plant health. The technology can use sound, pictures and graphics to overcome the problem of illiteracy which has impeded so much learning until now.

Better use of mass communication media and new digital technologies will neither make field workers redundant nor remove the need for face-to-face contact. As with the teachers mentioned above, it will change the role of field extension workers and increase their efficiency. It will help farmers to use the technology to identify their individual problems and to work out individual solutions. Field workers, instead of acting as postmen/women for delivering information, will become local managers of learning and communication processes. In the health sector, for example, a recent unpublished study by the Ministry of Health in

India found that health workers were spending a minimum of 40 per cent, and some as much as 75 per cent, of their time filling in forms and writing reports. Selected clinics were provided with simple computers programmed to streamline such work. This reduced time spent on administrative work to 13 per cent (and paid for the computers in eighteen months). A programme in Peru has shown how computers at village level can transform the role of health workers in community health.[8]

Examples already exist in isolated initiatives all round the world which, separately, demonstrate how the technology can be used at village level for a wide range of different purposes. A feature of these programmes, however, is that virtually none has spread widely. Problems of cost, of both hardware and software, and needs for electricity, maintenance and skilled support have prevented them from doing so.

A recent advance in the United States points the way for overcoming these problems. It has established a basis for the widespread expansion of these successful but isolated initiatives. It has beaten the barrier of the capital cost of digital technologies for those who have had no access to them until now. This advance is described in Chapter 4 but, before exploring its details and applications, there is a different issue that needs our attention.

Such advances enable new thinking and approaches for the whole process of information exchange and learning for health, agriculture, urban and rural development and much else. But this cannot be achieved within existing systems.

The fragmentation problem

The fragmented approach to development communication referred to at the beginning of the chapter is now affecting approaches to the use of new information technology by governments and donor agencies. As computers have become available, managers in each separate discipline have asked: 'What can a computer do for my office/research station/hospital/classroom/university/cooperative?' Now networks have arrived and each agency is again approaching the use of these on an individual basis – again funded by competing donor agencies or influenced by different hardware or software suppliers. This has been possible in the absence of policies and guiding conventional wisdom to direct otherwise.

The results are costly duplication and under-utilization of the existing equipment, and growing disenchantment with the technology. An environment of thought is needed in which the *generic* nature of digital technologies is recognized, in the same way that the generic telephone is recognized now. This will permit a *holistic* approach to the use of the new technologies – and other mass communication media – and will also show how to overcome the current fragmentation of the communication process needed for the development of people. This is the subject of the next chapter.

Conclusion, Part I

If Dr Soedjatmoko is right in concluding that development is, above all, 'the learning needed by individuals, communities, and nation states to prepare themselves to live in the future', and if development experience shows that the systems in place for development are not able to achieve the communication needed for that learning, then those systems are themselves part of the problem of development.

Conventional, 'mainstream' approaches to development have (inadvertently) attempted to make each technical sector and subsector its own communication channel, using people as their primary communication medium. In doing so, they have fragmented the communication process for development. Those systems and approaches have failed to achieve the human/social objectives of the various technical disciplines in which 'development' has been organized. Moreover, those systems are also unable to achieve the two-way communication and learning needed in the fields of 'new' priority, which governments and humanity now face, and which do not correspond to the mandates and staff skills of traditional technical sectors.

Interactive, digital technologies introduce new tools of enormous potential for addressing communication, learning and local empowerment. These technologies, and the new perceptions of the roles of information and communication in development, will introduce approaches that will enable development to move beyond the confines of current orthodoxy. They will help us to see and to accept that information and communication systems have an identity in development which is different from that of the conventional perceptions within which most development

assistance to date has been planned and justi
profound implications for addressing the 'missin
government-led development to date: the means
people.

Part II of this chapter examines the nature of new
of communication systems and of the communication sector, and
a developmental role for the information industry.

II

If it is logical to invest in education systems to provide the
information and learning for children and adolescents in
schools and colleges, it is equally logical to invest in other forms
of communication systems to provide the information and
learning needed by adults, and by children out of schools.[9]

COMMUNICATION SYSTEMS

The familiar communication systems – telephones; radio and TV;
film and video; postal systems; books, newspapers, magazines and
other printed media – can serve all disciplines and technical
sectors equally. They are all generic. We do not need one
telephone line or radio transmitter for daily news, one to carry
information for agriculture, another for health, and more for
other topics. This contrasts with the parallel, technical field
services of most third world governments (discussed in Part I)
which have each attempted, effectively, to become its own
communication channel.

Traditional communication systems are less familiar to
non-third world people, even to most of those with experience of
living and working in the third world. Story tellers, theatre groups,
choirs, puppeteers and drums all have important roles in many
traditional societies. These are also generic, in that they can be
used to convey information on a wide range of subjects. Innovative
programmes have shown how to strengthen these systems.

There is one medium of communication that cannot be
generic. This is narrowly trained human beings who have only
specialist knowledge and skills in their specific professional fields.
Ironically, it is to this medium that most communication for
development has been entrusted in third world countries.

Roads, railways, canals and airlines carry goods of many kinds and for many purposes. Together, these systems comprise the transportation 'sector'. Similarly, communication systems can be thought of as highways – for carrying information of many kinds and for many purposes. The different communication systems together constitute the communication sector. Conventional wisdom for development has recognized the transport 'sector', but not the communication 'sector'.

In improving transport systems, their range and condition, their institutional requirements for operation and maintenance and their needs for improvement have been assessed. Their economic value has been calculated and they have had a place in macro-economic planning. We can regard communication systems in the same way.

We can assess the range and condition of each communication system in any geographic area, just as we do with roads, railways or canals. We can assess their institutional requirements for effective operation. We can justify investment in their coordinated improvement for the purpose of developing people and institutions, and give them their place in economic plans. We have thought of telephone systems and, to a lesser extent, broadcasting systems in this way. But their developmental roles have been at the fringe of the thinking within which most people and agencies involved in development have been operating. The problem has been compounded by the difficulty that economists have in allocating economic values to information, communication and learning.

Computers, networks and data bases have introduced new media for communication and learning. But advances in digital technology are doing more than this: they are merging many of the familiar communication channels. Digital telephony and broadcasting can use the same satellites, transmitters and receivers or the same optical cables. Data compression can combine voice and video signals so that TV and telephones can merge. Digital printers can be linked by telephone to remote desk top publishing. All this calls for a holistic approach to the communication sector to take account of these interfaces.

THE COMMUNICATION SECTOR

The nature and components of the communication sector are indicated in Table 2.1. This shows the sector's many parts and, by

Table 2.1 The communication sector

Communication channels	Information technologies	Information storage	Institutional requirements
Broadcasting: Radio, TV	Radio/TV hardware Production Transmission	Tape/records/ video	Radio/TV industries Programme production Broadcasting companies
Cable TV	Cable	Video	Cable companies
Print	Printing/publishing Micropublishing Microform	Books/magazines/ Newspapers/ directories	Publishing companies Libraries/archives
Post	Mail equipment		Postal services
Film/video	Film/video	Film/video libraries	Film production companies/cinemas/ distributors
Telephone	Telephony/fibre Satellite Mobile services		Telephone companies
Value added carriers	Networks Fax/Teletex/ E-Mail	Data bases	Information providers Software producers
Computers	Computer production Software production Multi-media	Disk/mainframe CD-ROM	Computer industry Software producers Information managers
Human: Teachers Field workers Management trainers Traditional: theatre/story tellers/music	Knowledge assessment Communication design/ management Assessment/design		Education services Advisory services Management companies Traditional systems Skills in research/ design/training
Value added services	Entertainment Advertising Distance learning		

implication, the sets of activities needed for their development. It indicates the physical infrastructure specific to individual communication systems. Development of that infrastructure is clearly outside the mandate of ministries of education, agriculture, health and irrigation or of local government. In addition, just as road and railway systems require institutional structures, administration, laws and appropriate skills for their operation, so too do communication systems. The fragmented approach to the development and use of mass communication systems, described in the last chapter, has failed to give adequate emphasis or resources to the institutional structures required to integrate the use of mass communications systems into both governmental and non-governmental services.

Important implications from Table 2.1 include the following.

1   Governments and donor agencies need guiding policies for the whole sector.
2   Partnerships are required between governments and the information industry to develop the communication sector.
3   Skills and manpower are likely to be the greatest constraints on realizing the sector's full potential in all developing countries. These, therefore, need to be given the highest priority for new investment.
4   Although most of the items in Table 2.1 are the physical elements of the sector, these comprise only the skeleton. The flesh is the information and the learning and management materials that the communication systems can convey. The ability to identify information and learning needs and to produce high quality materials in appropriate form are at the core of the communication sector.

Successful approaches to addressing individual parts of the communication sector are demonstrated in isolated programmes throughout the world. These show the independent identity of those systems and their parts and are proof that they do not 'belong' to any individual technical sector. Examples illustrate the point.

A programme in Ecuador, funded by USAID, strengthened the capability of a Communication Unit within the Ministry of Agriculture to assess farmer knowledge and skill needs, and to develop communication and training materials to help the Ministry to address those needs. The results were impressive.

Other ministries sought the media unit's assistance. The unit moved from being a single-sector to a multi-sectoral service. Government and NGOs paid for the services, eventually enabling the unit to become self-financing.[10] The same thing happened in Lesotho, but in this case it grew from an initiative in the education sector. A study found more than seventy different organizations in that small country which were involved in communication and behaviour change. Fewer than half of them were governmental. All needed the skills and services that the unit provided, but lacked those skills themselves.[11] Equivalent experience in other countries confirms the cross-sectoral need for this component of the national communication sector.

The Development Training and Communication Project funded by UNDP in Thailand went further than the Ecuador and Lesotho models. Beginning from supplying similar communication inputs for a population programme, the project expanded to provide training in the skills required to assess farmer needs and to produce training and communication materials. It also trained field staff and managers to improve their understanding of the management of the communication processes and behaviour change needed to achieve their various goals. Input from this programme spread to other countries, from Pakistan to the Philippines. This included support for projects in population, agriculture, livestock, forestry, health and nutrition, and even strengthened local government – again demonstrating the cross-sectoral need for, and nature of, this element of the communication sector.

Significantly, key people designing and implementing these and other similar programmes have been predominantly communication specialists, anthropologists, sociologists, training specialists, social researchers, adult educators and management trainers. All are disciplines that have little place in existing technical ministries, planning offices, ministries of finance and the major donor agencies. Recognition of the communication sector will provide a long overdue 'constituency' for the social skills needed to achieve the development of people and institutions.

Inadequacies in approaches to the development of the social sector are not confined to third world countries. In the UK and other European countries, reforms in educational and health services and penal systems are at the top of the political agenda. In the United States, $350 billion are spent annually on the public education system – $100 billion more per annum than was spent ten years ago – yet the statistics on student performance in the US public schools have not improved. Inadequacies of health and penal correction systems are common in developed and less developed countries alike. With increasing crime, there is direct conflict in the allocation of scarce resources between (a) the short term need for more jails for the growing criminal population, and (b) the longer term need for better training and education to keep young people off the streets and out of jail. In many countries the short term need is receiving priority, partly because it has been clear that marginal increases in investment in existing educational systems do not offer the solutions needed.

Part of the problem has lain in the conventional equation of learning and 'education' (meaning schools, textbooks, teachers and examinations). With new perceptions, we can see the relation between learning and communication. We can see that traditional education systems are a subset of the communication sector. They are a form of communication that can now be superseded by more modern and efficient forms. As indicated in the last chapter, we can change traditional education and field advisory systems – and overcome their inherent confines.

There is much more to new perceptions of information and the communication sector than its applications in the field of learning. Three diverse examples illustrate this: management information systems; rural credit and savings; and the future role of entertainment.

Management information systems

Up-to date information is critical for effective management. An early application of computers was the use of their data storage and processing capability for management. A large body of software now exists for management information systems in a wide range of applications. The eruption of sales of lap-top and now notepad computers testifies to the importance for management purposes of the portability of information that the technology has introduced.

Most computers in offices have been used largely as add-ons to traditional office practices. Their capacity to process data at accelerating rates has led to big increases in the production of unimportant information and the consumption of paper in large organizations, and to an increase in the bureaucratization of those organizations. The intention of the introduction of the technology was usually the opposite of these three outcomes. It is possible to prevent this – but it requires a different perception among office-based workers of the nature of 'work'.

Most people's work advances by building walls, digging holes, driving trucks, operating cash register machines, and the like. This is not the case with the work of, particularly, managers, supervisors and planners. Their work advances by agreements, decisions and commitments in relation to specific objectives. One or two innovative computer-based management information systems have recognized this. Their software requires managers and supervisors to focus constantly on agreements, decisions and commitments needed in relation to each specific objective and task for which they have responsibility. The software requires managers and supervisors to record and circulate (by electronic mail), to all involved in individual tasks, the outcome of every new agreement, decision and commitment relating to each particular task. Similarly, all members of teams working on specific tasks are required to enter information on their agreements, decisions and commitments where these affect the progress of the tasks. The system can, of course, also convey relevant background data needed for these management actions.

Substantial reductions in ineffectual meetings and circulation of paper have been achieved in organizations where staff have received training to give them a different perception of the nature of their 'work', at the same time as new technology and software have been introduced. Increases in efficiency and staff morale have also resulted. Moving information about decisions and actions that advance team work is another dimension of information and communication which has much potential that has yet to be exploited.

Credit and savings

When we write cheques, use credit cards or keep accounts, we do not move money, we move information about money. For those purposes, money and information about money are synonymous. The advent of technology that can move information anywhere on demand can help banks to overcome their most intractable obstacle – that of communicating with very large numbers of poor and illiterate people. Moreover, that same technology can read finger prints; it can inform illiterate people of their balances, due dates and options verbally or in pictures or graphics. Its processing and interactive capability also enables the technology to help individuals, groups and communities to manage their own finances.

Most of the increasing numbers of poor people in the world have no savings. For them, access to credit is a distant dream. They are all trapped in a cycle of poverty from which they are unable to escape. There are a few exceptions that show that solutions are possible. The Grameen Bank in Bangladesh is one. In an innovative approach, the bank made credit available to very poor women in rural communities. After five years, the comparative credit repayment figures in Bangladesh were: for commercial credit, 19 per cent; for agricultural credit, 28 per cent; and for repayment by the very poor, 98 per cent.

Other isolated programmes, such as that of the Canara Bank outside Bombay, the Pakistan Rural Credit Programme and the Savings Stamp programme in Zimbabwe, show that poor people will accept and repay credit if it is made available to them in a form appropriate to their needs and local management capacity. They show that the problem has not been the creditworthiness of the poor, but the inability of orthodox (western) banking systems to adjust to the needs of the poor. A difficulty for these banks has been the costs of reaching and lending to large numbers of poor people who each borrow very small amounts.

A system that can make the communication, processing and interactivity of digital technologies available at village level will provide a means of replicating on a large scale the successes of isolated programmes referred to above – and many others.

A recent study of computerization in banks in the UK concluded that the technology had increased substantially banks' capacity for handling banking transactions, but many innovations had failed to meet their full expectations. Generally, the study found that banks are becoming increasingly cautious of new investment in technology. The impact of the technology on the nature of jobs and of the psychology of the banking profession had been underestimated and was little understood.

None the less, the technology is moving on and major banks in more advanced information economies are progressing towards their objectives of 'home banking' and electronic funds transfer at the point of sale. The latter could largely replace cheques and even credit cards – once comprehensive participation is achieved by buyers and sellers alike. Their uses for credit, savings and financial management are important elements in holistic planning of information and communication systems.

Entertainment

A recent study in the USA found that, by the time the average American child has completed six years of primary education, he or she has spent in the region of 13,000 hours in school. Out of school, he or she will have also spent in the region of 17,000 hours watching television (and will have witnessed approximately 55,000 murders in the process!).

Traditional approaches have drawn strict boundaries between 'education' and 'entertainment'. More and more educators in the USA and elsewhere are asking what could be achieved if a modest percentage of television viewing by children could directly support school-related learning. What is the educational role of this medium? We can now go further than this.

A single informatics system which can provide information, education and entertainment materials on demand can both transform the present fragmented approaches to learning and help to break down the present barriers between 'education' and 'entertainment'.

Although TV is a sophisticated and expensive technology, it is already familiar to a great many poor people in developing countries. In the more community-orientated cultures of Eastern Asia in particular, wealthy villagers who own television sets often place them with the screen facing out of their houses rather than into them. People from the community can enjoy the entertainment and the TV owner's status is enhanced by doing this. In Senaa, the most northern and remote Governorate of Yemen, where many ancient traditions remain little changed, few families are now without video players and TV monitors. One finds tents in the desert with TV aerials. In these situations innovations in educational approaches are likely to more readily accepted than in the more entrenched conditions of Europe and North America.

All of this provides a basis to move our thinking beyond the guiding principles that have brought us to our present point in development. Recognition of the communication sector and holistic approaches to its development will draw the vast resources of the information industry from the peripheral role that it has had in 'development' until now into a directly developmental role. It will make the strengthening of countries' information industries an object of major new investment.

THE INFORMATION INDUSTRY

In the preoccupation of third world development with physical and economic objectives, the information industry has been made more a spectator of, and commentator on, events than an important player in achieving development objectives. The structural divisions between the subsets of the industry, shown in Table 2.1, have contributed to this, as has the lack of an environment of thought in governments and donor agencies in which to harness the resources of the industry for development.

The information industry has many different specializations: computer companies; telecommunication companies; companies specializing in satellites, software, advertising, printing, radio and TV, and so on. It has been outside the boundaries of the roles, staff skills and financial resources of any one of these subsets to tackle the combination of applications of mass communication media for their public use. The fragmentation in current praxis in approaching the communication process in development has caused a lack of sponsorship in governments and the donor community to integrate these different specializations in national plans for strengthening countries' communication capacity for development. Policies and guidelines are needed for doing this.

Several third world countries have begun drawing up national informatics policies. So far, these have been heavily oriented towards the traditional markets for the industry in commerce, business, services and government. They take on a major new dimension when seen in the context of the whole communication sector: the public uses of the new technologies and their integration with existing communication channels.

The primary markets in the developed economies for the western and East Asian electronic industries are now generously supplied. These industries are looking to the third world countries for further expansion. This offers to governments opportunities for harnessing new resources and for creating partnerships in developing their own information industries and communication sectors.

Many of the most innovative and successful uses of private sector expertise in mass communication media have been in the smaller sectors – health, population and nutrition, for example – which have lacked large cadres of field staff. Most recently, AIDS and environmental education programmes demonstrate this well. These have drawn upon the advertising industry in using social marketing approaches and have shown the potential of broadcasting and other news media in directly developmental roles. These examples indicate ways in which the communication skills and resources of the private sector can be drawn into directly developmental roles – and create new markets by doing so.

An institutional problem

Most of the experience referred to in this chapter is still fragmented. Governments and donors lack policies and organizational structures with skills and budgets to draw together experience in the communication sector and to replicate it widely. Where expertise and communication capability has existed, it has generally been located in small, inconspicuous units within individual technical ministries. The same applies in individual Technical Agencies of the United Nations. Staff in these small units live and work in a state of inevitable frustration, each seeing the need to develop generic communication systems in the countries in which they work but unable to do so because this is outside the mandate of their particular ministry or Technical Agency.

The communication professionals in the Technical Agencies have looked to the World Bank and the Regional Development Banks, with their mandate for assisting member nations' cross-sectoral planning for development. Those agencies have a leading role in policy dialogue with their member countries and in initiating new investment in the communication sector.

Ironically, the international development banks have been even more poorly equipped to perform this function than the UN Technical Agencies – in terms of both their staffing and their concepts of 'development'. In 1989, with the Information Revolution surging ahead, and with more than a decade of studies of development performance pointing to the inadequacies in, and need to address, the human/social ingredients of self-sustaining development, the institutional view of the world's leading development agency was still that 'communication is not a priority for this organization'. The problem is deep seated in what 'development' has been thought to be. We shall look into why this has happened in the next chapter.

A part cause and part effect of the problem has been the staffing of the technical ministries of governments and their counterparts in the donor agencies. For example, in 1986, after a decade of investment in 'agriculture and rural development to alleviate poverty' as its highest priority, the World Bank had 460 staff positions to handle its portfolio of 600 agricultural and rural development projects. The composition of those staff positions was as follows:

Technical specialists, e.g. agronomists, livestock specialists, irrigation engineers, foresters	180
Economists and financial specialists	270
Statisticians, cooperatives, marketing, and monitoring specialists	9
Sociologists	1

The World Bank has never had a position for a professional communication specialist among its staff to plan and supervise the communication needed in all of the agricultural and rural development projects that it funded.

The problem has not been restricted to the agricultural sector or to the World Bank. The number of positions for communication specialists and other social skills in the technical ministries of governments and in the donor community is extraordinarily small – in relation to the objectives of information transfer and behaviour change among billions of people in the programmes that those agencies support. UNICEF stands out as an exception in this regard, having more positions for communication specialists than almost all of the rest of the UN technical agencies combined. It is no coincidence that UNICEF programmes have achieved a high record of success in changing behaviour at community level.

USAID has also funded much innovative work in development communication. Its organizational structure includes a Science and Technology group with this expertise and responsibility, able to work across technical sectors. The exceptions indicate the internal, institutional nature of the inability of agencies with poor track records in addressing the human dimension of development.

The World Bank's March 1992 Policy Research Bulletin begins with the statement: 'More than natural resources, more than cheap labour, more than financial capital, knowledge is rapidly becoming the key factor of production.' This new appreciation of the importance of knowledge in development is welcome but, more importantly, the paper does not go on to the next logical step of advocating investment in the communication systems (and the communication sector) to transfer knowledge.

The neglect of the communication process and of communication systems to develop people is an extraordinary, global phenomenon. Its pervasiveness indicates a fundamental problem. It is important to know why this neglect has come about. This is the subject of the next chapter. After that, we can explore some of the exciting advances that new concepts and communication technologies are introducing and how they will enable development to break out of the confines of present traditions.

CONCLUSION

'Development' is about the development of people as well as about addressing their physical needs. If it is logical to invest in education for the information and knowledge needed by children and adolescents, it is equally logical to invest in communication systems for the information and knowledge needed by adults and by children not in school. Communication systems, like transport systems, form part of the infrastructure for development. Their role is the development of people. Different communication systems together form a sector with its own place in macro-economic planning. This has not been part of the conventional thinking in which development has been approached, nor are the structures currently in place for development adequately staffed or organized in this field. Different perceptions of information and of the communication sector are possible and needed. They open up a wide range of new opportunities. They provide a basis for drawing the resources of the information industry into the mainstream of development and of advancing development to a new era. We need to understand why has this not happened sooner. This is the subject of the next chapter.

Chapter 3

Why?

In understanding a tradition, the first thing to be aware of is
how it is concealed by its obviousness.[1]

Twenty years ago, two men stood at a high vantage point in the
foothills of the Drakensburg Mountains in Lesotho. They
overlooked the catchment area of the Little Caledon River to the
west and south, extending down to the outskirts of the capital,
Maseru, and that of the Phutiatsana River running northwest past
Teya-teya-neng. They had been siting rural access roads, bridges,
markets and new staff houses as part of the country's first large
scale rural development project. The project would fund rural
infrastructure, agricultural inputs, credit, advisory services, farmer
training, livestock improvement, soil conservation, vehicles and
equipment, additional staff and other components in an
integrated approach to develop the whole catchment of the Little
Caledon and would benefit the 17,000 farming families living
there. Both men were agriculturists. One, a Masotho, was a senior
official of the Ministry of Agriculture with many years' field
experience throughout the country. The other was much younger;
he was from the UK and was employed by FAO to assist with this
new venture.

Pointing out an area towards Teya-teya-neng, the Masotho said,
'Some years ago, a donor agency funded a project in that area. It
was like the one that we are planning now. You can see that
nothing remains.'

The younger man responded by saying that the new project
would be different. It was based on much experience from similar
programmes in other countries funded by many international
agencies. It would not be an isolated project like the previous one

but would be the start of a long term programme of integrated development that would spread to other parts of the country.

The Masotho shook his head. He said that he feared that the outcome would be the same. When pressed to give reasons for his forebodings, he could not do so – particularly in English. Had he been able to, the younger man would probably not have been able to accept his reasoning.

The project was funded by a combination of donors and proceeded as planned. Much activity was created; much enthusiasm and support were shown by the local people and government authorities; a lot of money was spent. Today, the physical infrastructure remains and some benefits can be shown but, for most people living in the area, the results of that investment are as the older man predicted. Much professional effort and good intention was in vain. Why?

In India, for a decade from 1977, the World Bank funded a series of projects to strengthen agricultural advisory services in different states. These projects improved management and staff training of existing services, added more staff, increased their mobility and trained 'contact farmers' – all of this to improve the communication of technical information to farmers. Over most of the same period, from a different pocket, the World Bank funded rural telephone services so that there are now working telephones in approximately 400,000 villages in India. The telephones introduced a new means of communicating with the villagers. We can examine the design of the agricultural projects to see how later ones changed over that period to reflect this significant change in the means of communicating with the villages. One finds no change in the design whatever. No use of this new communication medium was built into the later projects. Why?

Development of any kind involves change. Change itself involves new knowledge, perceptions, skills and activities. Evaluation of development performance worldwide over the past two decades has shown persistently that the communication needed to change behaviour, particularly among the poor, has not been achieved. Yet, as mentioned in the last chapter, the institutional view of the world's leading development agency at the end of the 1980s was still that 'communication is not a priority for this organization'. Why?

Questions like these abound in assessments of development experience in all developing countries and in all major donor agencies. Meanwhile, the marginal returns from investing in more educational, agricultural or health projects on conventional lines are getting smaller. The numbers of people in absolute poverty continue to increase. These and other persistently elusive goals of development indicate a fundamental problem in approaches to date for achieving self-sustaining development and poverty alleviation.

The unresolved problems of development derive not so much from the nature of the undeveloped countries and their people as from the inadequacies of conventional approaches to assist them. Einstein said: 'The thinking that has brought us to our present stage cannot carry us beyond it.'

If we are to advance beyond our present stage in development, our thinking must advance. A pervasive cause underlying the sorts of problems alluded to above is inherent in the nature of most professional people working to achieve development. It lies in their backgrounds, their professions and the language of their professions, e.g. scientific, economic, financial or legal. All of these have 'programmed' their thinking and reasoning. Conventional perceptions have set the confines of the existing institutions and approaches that we have created for development. The following sections examine how this has come about.

AN UNDERLYING PROBLEM

We all, naturally, seek solutions in our own fields of specialization and through the organizations and institutions within which we work. Financiers look for solutions in more money; agriculturists in seeds, fertilizers and cropping practices; engineers in new structures; economists in economic models and so on. Information is generated and received within each discipline and sector. Budgeting processes, existing mandates and staff profiles perpetuate existing organizations. We all accept information that reinforces our current way of thinking and reject information that appears to undermine it. These and other forces tend to maintain the status quo. Few people are rewarded in governments, large bureaucracies or academia for questioning traditional disciplines and existing organizational structures. To suggest that conventional disciplines and the organizations in place for development are themselves a part of the problem of development is heresy!

When we allow ourselves the luxury of questioning conventional thinking and its inherent confines, we find answers to some of the questions posed above – and exciting new possibilities emerge.

Confines of thinking and language

The next section comes from work led by Professor Richard Bawden, now Principal of Hawksbury College at the University of Western Sydney and from the author's subsequent contacts with Professor Bawden's work.

While working initially with agricultural pharmaceutical companies and then with FAO, Professor Bawden noticed that a minority of agricultural extension agents were much more successful in influencing farmers than others. A majority of agents, in more developed and less developed countries alike, were remarkably ineffective. He saw the same phenomenon in Australia when he joined the staff of the Queensland Agricultural College and decided to examine it further. He moved to Hawksbury College where, for seven years, he led a team exploring this subject.

The team began from the assumption that the less successful extension workers lacked agricultural knowledge and that better teaching of agricultural science was called for. This quickly proved unfounded. Looking further into the subject, it became apparent that the problem was not a technical agricultural one at all. It had to do with:

(a) Farmers' ability to receive and understand technical information;

(b) Their interpretation of that information in their own farming and social contexts – which were often different from the technocratic contexts in which the information had been generated (usually research stations);

(c) What seemed to agriculturists to be the farmers' 'irrational' decisions in not adopting improved methods.

The team showed that the language and reasoning used by the more successful agents was different from the others. It took account of the farmers' individual social considerations, while the language and reasoning of the less successful agents was much more confined to technical content and logic. Many of the better agents – but not all – came from farming backgrounds. It appeared that the farmers and the better agents *thought* differently from the less effective agents.

Delving further into the work of sociologists, anthropologists, philosophers, educators and neurologists, Bawden and his team found the causes of their findings. Their conclusions are summarized below.

THINKING STYLES

People from different backgrounds have different styles of thinking and reasoning. Everyone has a dominant style which can be shown by modern testing techniques. In their simplest form, these can be described as follows.

Holistic

The term 'holistic' is used here in its simple sense – as the opposite of 'reductionist' and as a 'multi-disciplinary' thinking style. Everyone starts life equipped to think holistically. People in simple societies continue to think in a holistic style. Kalahari bushmen, to take an extreme example, are neither botanists, zoologists, entomologists, soil scientists, hydrologists nor weather forecasters but have more usable knowledge of each of these fields and of the interactions among them as they apply to their way of life than most professionals in any of these disciplines.

Young children learn holistically. At home and in kindergartens one can watch them explore their environment and apply quite naturally their new discoveries in one field to what they know in another. They fit each new piece of knowledge into their growing understanding of the world around them. Seymour Pappert's work at the MIT Media Laboratory and that of other leaders in computer-based instruction have indicated the potential of digital technology for assisting in experiential learning. By permitting children to learn in their own ways, customized learning can help and encourage children to explore knowledge; it can help them to link knowledge with relevant principles and concepts and to guide practical exercises through which learners can apply their knowledge and concepts and so fully understand them.

Good teachers can do this when they are able to give their full attention to small groups of children. However, good teachers are too scarce and too expensive for the numbers required to provide customized instruction everywhere.

Reductionist

At age five or six, children are sent to school. There the body of knowledge to be taught is so great that it has to be categorized for the convenience of the teacher and to make organized learning manageable and examinable. Knowledge is reduced into convenient subjects and disciplines. As education proceeds, more and more is learned about less and less. The disciplines develop an identity of their own and lock knowledge into compartments. Our education systems have created our conventional disciplines and professions – and the barriers between them.

So, from our original, dominant, holistic way of thinking, our education converts us to a reductionist style of thinking. Our education and, later, our professional environments together programme us with the language, skills, reasoning and confines of our chosen field. In western countries, this is accompanied by a strongly rationalistic reasoning based on our mathematical and scientific culture. It programmes us to seek answers, not questions.

The reductionist style is superimposed on our innate holistic style – it does not totally replace it. This is indicated in Figure 3.1.

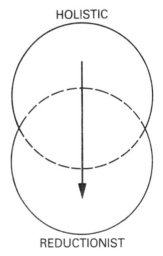

Figure 3.1 Holistic and reductionist thinking styles.

Practical or abstract

On completing their education, some people remain in academia or in purely scientific environments and retain very dominant reductionist thinking styles. Others move in one of two directions. Some may make their lives in the practical working world – in business, commerce, services, farming – where they face real life situations every day which require them continually to cross the boundaries between conventional disciplines. Their style of thinking moves from reductionist to 'practical' as their experience grows – although most people remain strongly confined in their activities and reasoning by the language and skills of their professional training and the nature of their jobs.

Alternatively, some are equipped by their education to move in the opposite direction: into fields dominated by 'abstract' thinking styles. Economists and lawyers are among this group. In their professional roles, they see the world through the filters of the rules, interpretations and languages created by their own disciplines. Their reasoning is justified within sets of rules of their own invention. Political ideologists do this too.

The four styles can be represented diagrammatically as shown in Figure 3.2.

The degree of dominance of any style of thinking varies among individuals. Through testing, one can position individuals on the diagram to reflect that dominance. Their position changes as they gain experience or are 'reprogrammed' by additional training.

There is a fifth thinking style and basis for reasoning. This is almost lost to a great many in western societies who now have difficulty in relating to it. This is a spiritualistic style. We can think of it as an extension of holistic thinking. It expands the nature of that holism. This style is strong in the more religious cultures of Asia and is particularly strong in Africa. It contributes to 'the reality of Africa' which few westerners comprehend.[2]

Superimposed on our individual style of thinking is our 'breadth of perception'. This too influences our language and our reasoning. Simple societies and children have a breadth of perception that is limited largely to their physical horizons. This expands with new knowledge, with travel and with broadening contacts and experience. Typically, professional staff working internationally have particularly well developed breadth of perception. Their language and reasoning may be almost

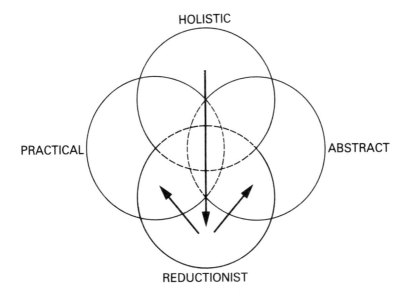

Figure 3.2 The four thinking styles.

incoherent to subordinate staff of government agencies with whom they come in contact!

APPLICATIONS

Agriculture

Professor Bawden and his team applied all of this to the training of agriculturists and have provided a basis for a review of traditional agricultural education which has worldwide applications. They have taught agriculturists to understand their own thinking styles and those of farmers and to recognize and understand the accompanying language, reasoning and decision making processes. This training equips students to understand the social factors that influence farmers' decisions. With this awareness, the students become much more effective field extension agents. The training has moved their 'programming' from the highly reductionist, technocratic product of traditional agricultural education back towards a more holistic and practical style of thinking.

Health

During a presentation discussing the global implications of Professor Bawden's findings for the training of agricultural field staff, a medical doctor commented: 'The situation is even worse in health.' This surprised other participants, since most people think of the health sector as a more human oriented field. The doctor pointed out the extremely technical, logical nature of medical training in which diseases, their symptoms and their treatments are each defined in a highly scientific, rationalistic manner. Doctors are taught to see the cause and effect relationship between, for example, a sore throat and staphylococcus and to think of the right amount of antibiotic as the satisfactory solution. We have the verbal distinctions for these things that our scientific knowledge has given us. There are African languages, however, which lack words for disease and for health. The cause of a sore throat in those cultures is clearly something that one has eaten or something that one has said. In this situation, there is a total misfit between western and traditional rationales. People's decisions and subsequent behaviour will be very different in these two environments of thinking. Communication and discussion are difficult, if not impossible, without the same verbal distinctions. Western-trained doctors, agriculturists, engineers and other scientific people are seldom equipped to deal with cross-cultural communication. In this situation, their natural course of action is to rely on their scientific solutions being superior. This has major implications for new training for field staff in all of the technical services – to equip them to deal with the communication processes involved in the behaviour change needed in their various fields.

An evaluation by the World Bank of the first 46 Health, Population and Nutrition projects it funded showed that, while the projects had been generally successful in establishing health structures, providing drugs and staff training and strengthening health ministries, they had all, with only two or three exceptions, had little success in changing health behaviour among intended beneficiaries.

Governments and donor agencies

Governments are organized in the familiar technical ministries and departments which correspond to the accepted disciplines. Each has its own work to do – often with little need for contact with professional disciplines outside the sector. The development agencies are structured in the same way, with the extreme form being the UN Technical Agencies with 'Agriculture' in Rome, 'Health' in Geneva, 'Education' in Paris and so on.

Each sector is staffed almost exclusively with professionals in its own disciplines – and thus equipped with the languages and mandates that go with them. The work of agriculturists, including what they read and write about and what society has expected from them, is in the language of soils, seeds, crop spacing, yields, crop and animal pests and diseases, fertilizers, tractors, etc. The language of engineers is in terms of structures, design, forces, stresses and strains, materials, tolerances, assembly, suppliers and maintenance. Economists think of supply, demand, incentives, prices, rates of return and economic models. Educational authorities are concerned with schools, curricula, textbooks, teachers, examination policies, educational advancement, drop out rates, internal and external efficiencies. It is in the language of our respective disciplines that we each approach our work. Note the physical emphasis of all of these.

Normally, one would not employ a professional in any of the above disciplines to do the work of another. One would not employ an agronomist to be a doctor, a lawyer to design bridges, or an economist to build a dam. They would lack the skills and language needed to do so. One would not employ any of these to achieve village mobilization, management training, local government or strengthening of communication systems, i.e to deal with the human and institutional development *functions* shown in Table 1.1. The reductionism of their 'programming' has not equipped them to be effective in these fields. So the almost exclusively technical, economic and financial staffing of the existing developmental organizations has pre-empted their ability to be effective in the human/social dimension of that development. (Which is not to say that they could not become competent in other fields with appropriate retraining.)

The degree to which the compartmentalization of knowledge and the dominance of technical, physical and economic priorities has excluded attention to the human dimension of development is extraordinary. Between 1976 and 1980, for example, in agricultural projects in which the World Bank invested $US920 million, not one cent was allocated for training for staff to implement any of them. (Most of these were large scale irrigation projects.) The technical specialists who designed the projects and their technical counterparts in government ministries had each dealt with the details of their respective physical components. It was outside the briefs of any of them to deal with the human and social aspects and these had no place in the calculations of the economic rates of return on which the projects were justified.

This omission of attention to the human dimension is a global problem. The phenomenon is well illustrated in an extract from an official statement of a country's national objectives after a period of devastating internal strife in the country. It is from an announcement by the President of the country following intensive negotiations between the government and international financing bodies.

> The thrust of our resource mobilization for economic recovery and for selected projects aims at concentrating action in the following key areas:
>
> 1 Acquisition of agricultural machinery and animal drugs.
> 2 Repair of both trunk and feeder roads.
> 3 Acquisition of commercial vehicles, spare parts and other supplies.
> 4 Acquisition of industrial raw materials and spare parts.
> 5 Rehabilitation of industries producing essential commodities.
> 6 Rehabilitation of public utilities.
> 7 Provide essential commodities, especially for health and education.
> 8 Development of construction capacity.

Note how the language of these objectives is exclusively physical. Language for addressing the human/social dimension of development is totally absent. This is despite the fact that recent war and an exodus of skilled people had severely depleted the country's human capital and that the political leadership was promoting community-based approaches for the country's recovery.

A study of the language of most countries' macro-economic

plans and of many development policy documents reveals the same phenomenon. Their language excludes attention to the human/social dimension of sustainable development – commonly, 'human resource development' is translated narrowly to mean basic education and basic health services.

Typically, objectives such as those in the example above are translated into budget allocations to the relevant technical sectors. Technical people prepare terms of reference for technical specialists to design and subsequently implement projects to accomplish physical objectives. The intentions of all concerned are to help the 'intended beneficiaries' but, as the wording above indicates, attention to the development of the beneficiaries' capacity to help themselves is often pre-empted from the outset.

A practical application of the problem is demonstrated by another example. The largest agricultural programme in the world under a single management is not to be found in the USA, Australia, Russia or China but in Africa. It is a huge irrigation programme in Sudan upon which over 1.5 million people are dependent. Major rehabilitation of the whole scheme was needed. Specialists were brought in from many parts of the world to help local teams to plan the repair and/or upgrading of canals, drainage systems, pumps, dams, sluice gates, the railway, the telephone system, cotton ginneries, vehicle fleets, mechanical workshops, schools, research stations and staff housing and to revamp accounting systems. Impressive documents were produced; a programme costing hundreds of millions of dollars was planned and a satisfactory economic rate of return was calculated on the investment needed.

It was only when final touches to the plans were being made, after two and half years' work, that someone raised serious doubts concerning the local capability to operate this massive programme. On investigation, it was found that of the 257 senior managers in the many different departments of the organization, only 29 would not have reached retirement status by the end of the initial five year project period. Of 151 agricultural managers, only one would not have reached retirement age.

The country had become independent some thirty years previously. Many positions held by expatriates had been localized. Employment on the scheme was prestigious and few had left. Young staff had all moved up the ranks together and virtually the entire senior management of the whole programme (and many of their immediate subordinates as well) were reaching retirement age at much the same time. The various technical specialists brought in to help to plan the rehabilitation programme had each examined and drawn up detailed proposals for their different components but, as technical people, their role had not been perceived to be an examination of how the whole programme would be staffed and managed. Their contributions had all been in technical and physical language and objectives.

A similar imbalance between resources allocated to the technical/physical and the human/institutional elements of project design can be shown worldwide.

Let us return to the beginning of the chapter and examine the examples there in terms of thinking styles and language.

The goals of the rural development project in Lesotho were defined almost exclusively in the physical terms that followed from the skills and reasoning of the agronomists, livestock specialists, roads and soil conservation engineers, marketing specialists, foresters and other technical people responsible for its design. Economic values were given to the incremental production, import substitution, soil retention, road access and other physical elements of 'production'. A positive economic rate of return was calculated and the investment was justified – and judged to be 'right'. Throughout, there was the implicit assumption that the farmers would accept new techniques, improved inputs, access to credit and economic incentives. Many of the project's objectives were accomplished but its design did not deal adequately with developing the capacity of the people – or of groups and communities – to adopt and maintain the changes. The project was not planned in the context of the social realities of the people whom it was intended to help.

The more holistic thinking of the Masotho told him that the physical and financial solutions being planned in the project – and even the farmer training that would concentrate on providing farmers with better agricultural knowledge – were insufficient to achieve the behaviour changes and local management capacity that purely technical and economic reasoning anticipated. But the Masotho was snared in the very trap that he was pointing out. His agricultural training and his whole working experience had equipped him to provide technical and physical remedies for agricultural problems. He could convert his agricultural remedies into specific plans and actions. His technical background had not equipped him to know of, or to design, the equivalent remedies for addressing the farmers' human/social constraints to behaviour change which he knew existed. He lacked adequate language to explain his doubts convincingly, particularly in English.

The western agricultural expert too, with his strongly technical, rationalistic background (reflecting the ruling conventional wisdom of the organizations in which he worked), was equipped to deal with and to value the development of agriculture but not the development of people. (The Lesotho project was one of a generation of similar integrated rural development projects which spread across Africa and to other parts the world from 1965 to 1985. Later projects paid greater attention to social considerations, staff and farmer training, communication processes and local government. The Proderith programme in the Proderith region of Mexico is perhaps the best example of success in addressing human/social development objectives on a large scale as part of a major integrated rural development project.)

The example of the telephones in India illustrates the effects of reductionist thinking in a different field. The telephones were put in by electronic engineers and linemen whose job was complete when telephones were installed and worked. They lacked the training, experience or mandate to show agriculturists how this communication medium could be used in the development of agriculture. The agriculturists, on their part, were concerned with crop and animal production and with increasing the efficiency of large numbers of agricultural field staff. It was outside their experience or training to integrate telephone communication into more comprehensive approaches for changing people's behaviour. Nor had their training oriented them to see their own role in a broader communication process.

In comparison, a private telephone company in Chile installed telephones in villages. To boost the use of their service, they made one line available to villagers free of charge for seeking agricultural advice. They employed a few agricultural staff at a central location to respond to the farmers' questions. Once villagers' initial diffidence was overcome, use of the service grew rapidly. It was extended so that difficult cases could be passed on to research workers directly. It supplemented and assisted the work of the agricultural field agents (it did not replace them) and subtly changed their roles. Instead of being the primary channel for delivering technical information, they spent more time helping farmers to identify their own, individual problems and in showing them how to use the phone to seek advice when they needed it.

The confines of the reductionism in our backgrounds keep appearing in development experience. Another example from India illustrates the point. Foresters are trained to manage and protect forests and forestry plantations. Traditionally, their product has been mature timber, requiring the trees to be widely spaced and given decades to reach maturity. Agronomists, on the other hand, deal with food and cash crops, mostly annual crops grown on arable land. Agriculture also encompasses tree crops and plantations, such as rubber, cocoa, coffee and oil palm. Here, too, mature trees are needed and are widely spaced. These are part of the parameters within which foresters and agronomists operate.

A retired doctor and a retired engineer in India each saw the strong market that existed for fuelwood and building poles. Independently, they both began experimenting with planting fast growing trees on irrigated land. They found that by spacing their 'trees' at 1-foot intervals, in rows a yard apart, they could grow a marketable product in three years. The net income exceeded almost anything else that they could grow on the same land.

The reaction of some senior government agronomists was: 'You can't do that! This irrigated land is for crops.' Similarly, planting trees a foot apart was outside most foresters' experience. Foresters and agronomists were both keenly aware of the fuelwood market, yet neither had been trained to think of trees as an arable crop. Neither had thought of this solution. The doctor and the engineer were not confined by conventions (the traditions) imposed by the agronomists' and foresters' professional training. They could 'break the rules' and treat trees as a short term crop. They created new opportunities by doing so, which led to major social forestry programmes in India and elsewhere.

COMMUNICATION AND ECONOMICS

The answer to the question posed earlier, as to why development communication has been neglected by most multilateral donor agencies, is complex. It derives in part from each technical discipline attempting to become its own communication channel (discussed in Chapter 2); from the assumption that investment to strengthen the conventional government field services will automatically improve their communication with intended beneficiaries; from the preoccupation of national planners with increasing GNP; and from the great difficulty that economists have in giving a value to information and to communication systems.

'Communication' has lacked a physical identity in the conventional way in which economists in government planning offices and donor agencies have thought about development. The convenient solution has been simply to leave it out of economic analysis. But there is a more fundamental problem.

The foundation of economics is the theoretical relationships between supply, demand and price (in perfect market situations). The 'imperfections' – or 'distortions' – of real world market conditions have given employment to larger and larger numbers of economists to produce theories and models to explain and allow for those imperfections and to predict accordingly.

Economics is a mathematical abstraction of reality. If the figures add up to 100 per cent, they must be 'right'. If they do not, economists look for and quantify, 'distortions' that will bring their totals back to 100.

'Perfect market conditions' assume perfect knowledge, skills, information and communication of information. In the simple market conditions in which economic theories were first conceived and in the industrialized countries in which they were developed and applied in earnest, the knowledge, skills and communication were generally adequate for supply, demand and price relationships to perform more or less as predicted. Advertising became a major industry and communication was not a major impediment, so communication systems did not feature in most economic planning. In that environment, it was possible for economic work to proceed as though information and communication systems were unimportant.

Established economic theories and practice were exported to less developed countries where the conditions of knowledge, skills and communication are substantially different. But this was not evident in the abstract world of economics where information and communication had had no place before.

All economists know of the dichotomy between the realities of the real world and the tidiness of their mathematical interpretations of those parts of it which they can measure. Without technical backgrounds themselves, development economists generally have had to take on trust the conclusions and solutions of the specialists in each technical discipline. The physical, quantifiable development priorities of the technical professions has suited the mathematical world of the economist. Without a constituency in either realm, the absence of 'communication' in the development recipe has not been missed.

The development solutions with which we have all grown up and which we have accepted unquestioningly are only part solutions. They do not have the validity that our programming has instilled in us. The sum of those parts, which had been thought of as adding up to 100 per cent, in fact adds up to only 80 per cent. (This will be discussed further in Chapter 5.)

When one accepts this argument, serious flaws appear in the economic reasoning and justifications on which much macro-economic planning and development investment have been based. This has the effect on economists of shaking the ladder on which they have been standing. The information revolution and recognition of the communication sector, which previous conventional wisdom for development excluded, moves the ladder to a new position.

Many development economists will resist any questioning of their theories and models. This is particularly true of development economists who lack practical field backgrounds to give them better understanding of different realities that do not match their abstract models. Such understanding would move their thinking style from the abstract towards the practical. Lack of it has contributed to the apparent blindness in government planning offices and international development organizations, now run largely by economists, to the central role of information, effective communication and the development of people in the development process.[3] Information and the means to communicate information have become as vital to the developed economies as electricity, water and gas and the means to produce and supply them. Curiously, economists, whose work and existence depends on information, have generally been slow to recognize the nature of the communcation process in development.

A different measurement

The insufficiency of current economic measurements of development and of the nature of a solution is demonstrated by the following example. A major development project had been designed in a Latin American country. On the basis of its technical content, market projections and economic rate of return analysis, the project had been judged suitable for World Bank investment of $US250 million. A unit within the World Bank had developed a technique for assessing 'institutional capacity'. This was applied to the major organizations which were to be responsible for the project. It showed that these organizations neither had nor could create in the timeframe proposed for the project the human and institutional capacity needed to handle a programme of this magnitude. The project was redesigned within the confines of existing human and institutional capacities. The scale of the project was reduced – with a saving to the country of $US100 million. (Similar results have been achieved on a smaller scale in several other countries.)

The economic justification based on physical and financial criteria was not wrong but was insufficient. A measurement of the human/institutional capacity was needed as well.

To estimate momentum, one needs two quite different measurements: mass and velocity. Neither measurement can be a substitute for the other and neither is adequate alone. One could consider the physical/financial/economic dimension of development to be its mass and the human dimension to be its velocity. If one skimps on the velocity, the mass will not have the momentum needed to achieve its objective.

A different perception is needed and is possible in yet another field: creditworthiness.

Creditworthiness

There is increasing questioning among prominent development practitioners and observers about the nature of creditworthiness. Creditworthiness has been judged in economic and financial terms. There is growing consensus that unless the product of an investment is sustainable over time in environmental terms, that investment is not creditworthy.

This brings us again to the relationships between (a) people and the environment, (b) people and the information and knowledge that they require to manage their environment, and (c) the communication systems they need to obtain that knowledge and information. People and institutions lacking the necessary information and skills are not creditworthy.

There may seem to be a conflict here with the experience

quoted above from Bangladesh and other places of very high credit repayment performance by the very poor – people generally thought to be uncreditworthy and with very limited sources of information. In fact, very poor people typically borrow very small amounts for activities that are well within their capacity to handle. Their families, groups or communities provide the surety which they lack and ensure that they borrow only for activities for which they have the necessary information and knowledge. It is the large numbers of the not so poor and the poorly educated, who are encouraged by banks and credit systems to borrow – often for activities for which they have insufficient skills and information – who so often prove uncreditworthy.

Conversely, investment to increase the availability of relevant information and knowledge when and where it is needed can improve the creditworthiness of both people and institutions.

CONCLUSION

This chapter has set out, very briefly for such an important topic, a basis for understanding the confines of thinking underlying the chronic difficulties that conventional development approaches have had in addressing the human dimension of self-sustaining development. This neglect of the human dimension of development in the technical, financial and economic traditions in which we have all been operating has been concealed by its obviousness.

The following is a statement by a President of the World Bank:

As the people of the world look back at the Development Decade, they feel a deep sense of frustration and failure. The rich countries feel that they have given billions of dollars without achieving [enough] in the way of Development. . . . There is no clear joint strategy for the future.

This could have been Lewis T. Preston, current President of the World Bank, looking back over the development performance of a great many countries during the 1980s. Actually, it was Robert McNamara in his first speech to the Board of Governors of the World Bank in 1968.[4] The fact that the statement is equally true today indicates that, despite significant annual increases in the scale of the investment for third world development during the intervening two decades, essential ingredients have continued to be missing from the recipe in use for achieving poverty alleviation and self-sustaining development.

Once we appreciate that the unresolved problems of development derive not so much from the nature of the undeveloped countries and their people as from the inadequacies of conventional approaches to assist them and that those inadequacies follow largely from the confines of prevailing thinking styles, we have a basis for questioning current orthodoxy. We have a basis from which to move beyond those confines and for addressing the elements of sustainable development which have been excluded by prevailing traditions. Digital technologies provide new tools with immense potential for helping us to do so. The next chapter examines the nature of these advances and their potential. It is now evident that there are no bureaucratic solutions to the structural problems of poverty, unemployment and the resulting inequities in the provision of essential services. The answer will have to come from a new partnership between the public and private sectors – for which informatics can provide an important tool.[5]

The next chapter describes concepts and new experience that demonstrate what this can mean in practice.

Chapter 4

Digital technology systems for public use

INTRODUCTION

> Computers will become a truly useful part of our society only when they are linked by an infrastructure like a highway system or an electric power grid. A National Information Infrastructure would be a common resource – like telephones are today.[1]

The information revolution is making new things possible that we could hardly have imagined even five years ago. Leading people in these fields tell us that we have seen only the beginning of what the technology holds in store. There is more to this revolution, however, than just the technology. In addition to whatever physical wonders it may perform, this new medium makes new thinking and approaches possible for addressing the whole human/social dimension of development. It will give new meaning to 'human resource development', 'human capital formation' and 'empowerment of people'.

This chapter does not require readers to be computer literate or to be familiar with the latest digital technologies. All that is needed here is to know that many kinds of information can be turned into electronic form, sent almost instantly from one place to another, and reconstituted immediately into a recognizable state at the receiving end. Alternatively, the information can be stored until needed either centrally or by end-users locally. The information can start off as sound, pictures, script, numbers or graphics – or any combination of these. It can be sent via telephone wires, optical cables, satellite or FM radio. It can be carried about on disks or tapes. It can be reconstituted as sound in telephone receivers, radios and CD players or as pictures on television and computer monitors; it can be projected on to screens or be printed by digital printers.

Add to this the processing capability of computers and the memory capacity of various storage technologies and we have tools for communication, interactive learning, management and entertainment that surpass anything that has existed until now.

All digital technologies are part of the same family. They can be combined into an 'informatics system' that can harness their multi-media capabilities. These systems will form part of the infrastructure for development in the future.

There are four other points to bear in mind. First, when 'computers' and 'computing' are mentioned, most people think of the now familiar personal computer (PC). The PC is a product of forty years of research and development that exploits the potential of computer technology for office use. In this form, interaction is through a keyboard or 'mouse'. The machine only occasionally uses its capacity to communicate in pictures. It almost never uses its capacity to communicate in sound. Had the object of the same forty years' development been to produce a computer that could communicate with illiterate people, its form would be substantially different from the conventional PC. It would interact with users mostly through touch screen technology; it would 'talk', using its capacity to transform digital information into sound; and it would communicate in pictures and symbols as well as in script. The technology already exists to do all of this.

Second, in discussing the role of digital technology in development, we are considering the future. Such a discussion needs to take place in the context of not only the technology we know today (much of which was designed a decade or more ago) but also the technology of the future and what it will soon permit.

Third, among the inputs needed for development, information in electronic form has a unique characteristic: it can be used without being depleted. If a charge can be recovered for such use, this has profound implications for the profitability of systems that can deliver digital information when and wherever it is needed.

Fourth, there was a decline of 50 per cent over thirty years in the cost of energy which fuelled the industrial revolution. There has been a continuing decline of 20 per cent annually over the past forty years in the real cost of storing, processing and transmitting a unit of information. This rate of decline is expected to continue.

I

A NEW TOOL

So far, most of the market for applications of digital technologies has been in industrial transformation, services (including financial services), public sector management and the military. Development of the technology has followed these markets. Many of these applications have required multiple access to distant data bases, e.g. keeping up-to-the-minute data on inventories and sales; checking credit cards; making airline reservations; and for many military applications. All of these have required centralized data and telephone infrastructure with very high switching speeds.

Many social applications of the technology have different needs. One can predict most of the software required in the short to medium term for many learning needs; for diagnosing human, animal and plant diseases; for land and environmental planning; and for a wide range of management purposes. Software for all of this can be located at local level and accessed at a fraction of the cost of retrieving it from central data sources every time that it is needed.

Commerce and industry have sponsored the development of the technology for their own applications. There has not been the equivalent sponsorship for the development of the technology for human and social applications. At the same time, only recently has the technology been sufficiently advanced or cheap enough to make its large scale use in the social sector economically feasible. Consequently, most people in the world have had little or no contact with and have not benefited directly from, the technology to date.

This is changing. Many programmes around the world have shown how computers can be used at village level and by illiterate people with no background in computer technology whatever. Some examples are as follows.

1   Buddhist monks in Bali are now managing a major expansion of their ancient irrigation programme with the help of Apple computers.
2   More than half of the school age children in Costa Rica have access to computer-based instruction through an IBM programme. Parents are now coming to the schools at night to

learn from the computers. The role and status of both the schools and the teachers in their communities have changed.

3   A health programme placed computers (powered by small solar panels) in remote villages in Peru. These helped villagers to keep their own demographic data and data on disease incidence and to diagnose seven common diseases. By compiling village data and helping villagers to interpret and understand that data, the technology promoted discussion and changes in group perceptions of health and disease. It led to new initiatives by the communities to take greater control over their own health-related activities and to new demands on the health service for their professional assistance in helping them to do so. It transferred initiative for health-related activities from the health service to the communities and achieved significant changes in health related behaviour.

4   Programmes in the Philippines and in India show a similar impact of the interactive capacity of the technology. It enabled villagers to enter and adjust data on their own physical, demographic and financial resources and to make group and community decisions on the basis of that processed data. Initiatives elsewhere have also demonstrated the technology's potential for helping remote communities to understand and manage their environment and to plan their own protection measures.

5   Interactive technology has been used successfully to train nomads from the Sahara, hill dwellers from Nepal, people from the paddy fields of Bangladesh and many others to operate complex oil drilling equipment in the Gulf. It also trains poorly educated GIs in the US military to operate and maintain sophisticated weaponry.

A few common findings from the rapidly growing body of experience in the use of interactive technologies include:

1   learners of all ages become processors of information, not just receivers;
2   instruction can be up-to-date and practice-related, rather than certificate oriented;
3   multi-media workstations and interactive video help to stimulate involvement through the manipulation of colourful images and displays, and live interaction with distant sites;

4   curiosity among learners rather than primary need become important driving factors;
5   student evaluation can be built into the software. In formal learning situations, this relieves teachers of wearisome hours of correcting written tests and makes them available for more productive teaching activities;
6   the technology is associated with progress. Access to, and familiarity with, it gives status to the users.

Lap-top and now notepad computers have introduced a new generation of applications all over the world. These include their use at village level for agricultural and health purposes, natural resource planning, credit and savings, and many other practices.

The technology is particularly good at assisting in interactive instruction in the maintenance and repair of machinery of all kinds, such as tractors, generators, water pumps and agricultural equipment in use at village level. It has great potential for introducing people to appropriate technology, such as solar energy, low cost pumps and building materials, and much else. The list of new applications in developing countries grows longer by the day. Governments of developing countries have already borrowed over $US700 million from the World Bank alone for information technology components in their projects.

A structural difficulty

So far, few of the many successful applications of the technology in the social sector have been replicated on a large scale. Each has been an independent, isolated endeavour by a different programme, company or institution. It has been beyond the role or resources of each separate initiative to expand its individual successes widely. The common problem has been that the limited range of uses of the technology in each case cannot justify either the capital costs of the hardware and software on a large scale or their on-going maintenance requirements.

The problem is evolutionary. Computers first became inexpensively and widely available for office use. Professionals in all fields – engineers, accountants, research scientists, educators, doctors, economists, agriculturists – have each, separately, asked the question: 'What can these computers or computer networks do for my office/laboratory/classroom/hospital/university/railway/ farm/company?'

Each different organization, government agency and profession has established its own data bases and networks – its own technology system – independently. The capital costs, maintenance and training implications of continuing to expand all of these parallel networks and narrow uses of network technology countrywide are too great for any one country. The equipment in many organizations is under-utilized and this is leading to a growing disenchantment with the technology. The approach is not sustainable.

A different approach is possible. This opens up what may prove to be the technology's largest market: its applications in the whole human/social sector of development, (namely its uses for interactive learning; communication; planning; management; credit and savings; and the empowerment of individuals, groups and communities for their own sustainable development. As this becomes widely understood and accepted it will introduce a new perception of the role and potential of information and communication in the development process.

Instead of asking what computers, data bases and networks can do separately for every different organization and discipline, we can now ask: 'What can a system combining the capacities of all digital technologies (an informatics system) do for all disciplines and sectors? What could a generic system do for the whole spectrum of information exchange, learning, management, financial control and governance needed for decentralized, self sustaining development?'

When we address ourselves to these questions, exciting new possibilities appear.

A SOFTWARE DELIVERY SYSTEM

Table 1.1 on page 8 shows the superior potential of a software delivery system (a digital system for public use) for assisting in a wide range of human/institutional development functions in which solutions have so persistently eluded governments and society worldwide. The following sections will address the questions:

(a) What is a 'digital system for public use'?
(b) What can such a system do?
(c) What are its costs and who pays for it?

(d) Who will own these systems?
(e) What practical experience exists in this new field?

The concept

A digital system for public use is an entirely new concept. It is possible to link the computing capability of computers; the local storage capacity of video, CD-ROM and magnetic and optical disk; the communication capability of telecommunication, FM radio and satellites; and the multi-media interfaces of displays, printers, CD players and projectors. They can all be combined into a single system to deliver digital information and interactive learning and management materials instantly as and when they are needed. The system can be operated and funded as a public utility – in the same way that electricity, water and gas utilities are operated today.

A principal feature is the decentralization to local level of very large memory and processing capability. This dramatically reduces the cost of accessing software and makes access to processing capability available to people and institutions who could not afford to purchase that capacity. For example, charges for access to central data bases in the United States currently vary between approximately $75 to $175 per user hour – much of which goes to the telephone companies through whose lines or satellite links the digital information has to travel. A new system now operating in the United States (the 'Education Utility', which is described below) has decentralized learning and management materials to storage located in individual schools and has linked this through a national 'gateway' to sources of other digital material which can be ordered and stored locally on demand. By doing so, the system has reduced the cost of accessing the material to less than 50 cents per user hour. This cost will be reduced further as technologies advance.

The software delivery system that this creates can deliver a very wide range of digital material for a very wide range of users and uses.

The central feature of shared usage of a single system which underlies water, gas and electricity supply utilities applies to software delivery utilities too. Water supply 'utilities' collect water in dams from large catchment areas, store it locally in reservoirs and tanks and supply it to users on demand. They establish the physical infrastructure and the organizational structures for doing so. Digital information and learning, management and entertainment software can be treated in exactly the same way. The software can be gathered from various sources, stored either centrally or locally and delivered to users on demand. The use of every item of software in the system can be metered and a small charge can be recovered for its use (part of which goes as a royalty to the producer of that software). If the numbers using the system are large enough, the system will be financially viable.

Various programmes have gone some way towards this. The 'Campus 2,000' programme in the UK links 10,000 schools to central data bases and permits all of the schools on the system to communicate with one another. The 'Teletel' programme in France has gone further, making small 'Minitel' terminals available to homeowners throughout France so that they can access information from central computers and use the 'Minitel' terminals for a limited range of software applications by the receiver. The 'Compuserve' programme in the United States offers a similar range of services available through modems to home-owned computers. These 'telematics' systems all rely on the telephone to access distant data bases where the main computing power is located. The 'Prodigy' educational programme, in wide use in New Zealand, does the opposite; it makes sets of educational software modules available to schools but lacks some of the communication features of the 'Campus 2,000' programme.

One can now marry the best points of all of these and go further. This is more than just attractive theory.

THE EDUCATION UTILITY: A WORKING MODEL

A working model already exists in the United States which has demonstrated the commercial viability of an electronic delivery system for formal education. The system, the 'Information and Education Utility', has been under development since 1981. It first became available in fully operational form in mid-1989 and has been introduced on a pilot basis in schools in Arizona, Utah, California and Florida. A brief description of how the Education Utility programme evolved may be helpful.

The approach was conceived by Jack Taub, inventor of the first computer data base – 'The Source'. He became involved in developing the computer-based education system, 'Plato'. From this background, he saw the potential of the technology for assisting children with learning difficulties and he addressed himself to the objective of providing customized education for all of them, using interactive learning materials.

There are approximately five million children with learning difficulties in the United States but a significant number of them are bright children who, as a result of their backgrounds or of very poor early experiences in school, are bored in the standard school system and become disorderly in class and rude to teachers. A solution is to label them as having 'learning difficulties'.

The underlying problem is not their learning disability but the inability of the conventional educational system to cope with learners from widely differing backgrounds and with disparate learning speeds and styles. Taub saw that the technology needed to provide educational materials for five million children with learning difficulties would be the same as that needed to reach all fifty million children in schools in the United States, and he set his sights on this larger goal.

The objective became to create a system that would:

(a) Realize the potential of interactive, digital technologies for delivering information and learning materials individually to the desk of every child in the United States;
(b) Permit all users to inter-communicate;
(c) Use the capacity of the same technology to assist the management and administration of schools and education systems;
(d) Be equally available to children at home and to other community users;
(e) Be affordable for poverty stricken education authorities.

Telecommunication, computing and storage (memory) technologies were already available with the capacity to do (a)–(d). Different programmes had produced educational software with demonstrated success in a variety of formal education applications. From earlier work with the Plato programme, the value of the integrated technologies to teachers and to the whole education process was apparent. The problem remained of how the expensive technologies could be made affordable.

The answer came when Taub recognized that digital information and learning materials can be treated like electricity or water and delivered by a new 'utility' system. The establishment of an 'education utility' system became the objective.

Point of departure

Here is the critical point of departure. By recognizing that digital information and software can be treated like water or electricity and by addressing that objective, one is no longer dealing with 'computers for education' in terms of formal education, distance learning or even 'education and learning' in their widest connotations. One is dealing with a new public utility and with the technology, infrastructure, finance, administration and maintenance needed to operate that system.

Once a software delivery system is in place, software already in use in a wide range of applications – education, health, farm management, local government, rural banking; administration of hospitals, research stations, cooperatives and irrigation infrastructure – can all be gathered together and distributed through that single, generic system. The 'electronic highway' that this creates will provide a means of spreading the many successful but isolated initiatives that already exist in different fields.

As soon as one moves from a 'computer in schools' approach to dealing with a new public utility, one moves from a focus on individual items of hardware and software for specific purposes to consideration of an open architecture system that is able to communicate with a wide range of existing hardware already in place in schools, offices, hospitals, homes and elsewhere. Such a system is not confined to a single operating system such as DOS or Apple Mackintosh. Its users may purchase whatever make of computer or other digital equipment that they like and link it into the system. Most hardware and software to date has been system-specific. Apple software has not run on IBM machines, for example and vice versa. A new generation of technology now makes it possible for an 'open architecture' system to 'speak' most modern computer languages and to inter-communicate among them. With the technologies' increasing power and sophistication, an open system will be able to accommodate virtually any modern hardware and software. The best high technology components and innovations available will be drawn into the utility system – just as they are with other utility systems now.

How the Education Utility system works

The system has three parts: a central store and gateway, local storage and processing capacity, and local access by users. The structure of the system and its configuration at a school site are illustrated in Figures 4.1 and 4.2. These show:

1 A central store from which most software regularly used by the system can be drawn. This central store (or 'National Resource Centre') is also a gateway to software producers, commercial data bases, video libraries, news agencies, government data banks and other sources of information and instructional, management and entertainment materials.

2 Decentralized storage and processing capability to which digital materials can be sent (down loaded) from the central store via satellite or land line for local storage. The local repositories (decentralized storage) can be located in schools, universities, hospitals, industries, local governments, military installations or wherever else the services are needed and sufficient subscribers can access the system. These local sites have very large digital storage and processing capacity – currently in the order of 30,000 megabytes – and will be larger in future versions. (All seventy books of the Bible, in digital form, occupy about 3.7 megabytes.) Additional software and topical information not stored locally can be ordered through the central store. Normally, down loading takes place at night to take advantage of low night time rates.

3 A local system through which to access the locally stored material and to supply it on demand to any user on the system. This could be a teacher, a student, a school administrator, the local educational authority, a parent or student at home, or business or other community users. Remote users can have access to the system through existing phone lines.

Through its command workstation(s) in each school, the system can deliver any piece of software from the school's digital stores to any terminal or group of terminals connected into local area networks. The system can currently manage up to 250 terminals from each command workstation, all of which are able to draw upon and work with, different items of educational software simultaneously. People with computers at home can connect into the system so that their children can continue to interact with the learning materials in the system from home. The system permits teachers to allocate learning materials to any student or group of students, individually and to check the students' progress with that

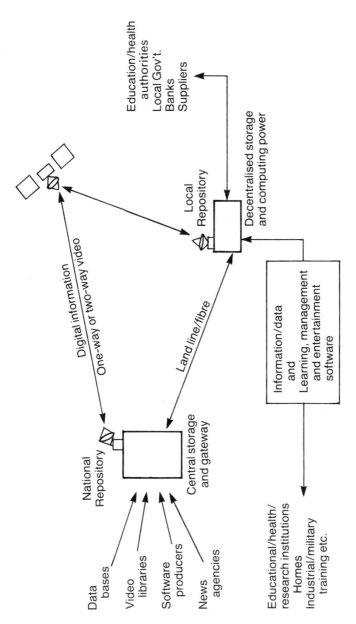

Data
bases

Video
libraries

Software
producers

News
agencies

National
Repository

Central storage
and gateway

Digital information
One-way or two-way video

Land line/fibre

Education/health
authorities
Local Gov't.
Banks
Suppliers

Local
Repository

Decentralised storage
and computing power

Information/data
and
Learning, management
and entertainment
software

Educational/health/
research institutions
Homes
Industrial/military
training etc.

Figure 4.1 Structure of the software delivery 'utility'.

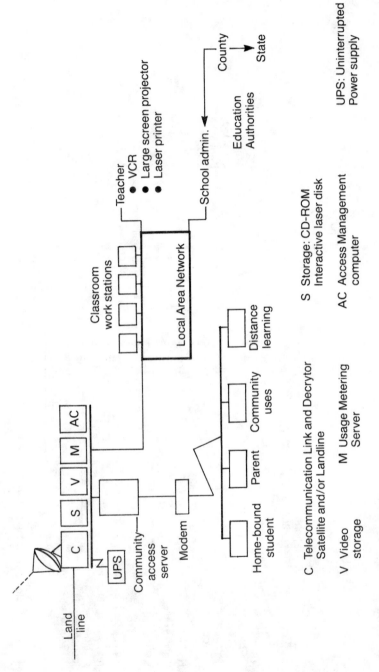

Figure 4.2 School site configuration.

software at any time. Teachers can do this from their classrooms, their offices or their homes.

The system meters the use of every item of software (in the same way that telephone calls are metered), so that users can be charged and a royalty for that use can be paid to the software producers.

Sophisticated mechanisms built into the system prevent piracy of software. With large numbers of people using the system, user charges can be very small and the system can still be profitable. Software producers can make their software available through the system at no cost to themselves and royalty payments for the use of their software are net profit. The reduction in packaging, marketing and distribution expenses is of great significance for relatively small scale producers. They need only make a single copy of their software available to the system. This overcomes a major problem for software producers of having large numbers of copies on the market which they have no way of protecting from piracy. Access to the system by poor or handicapped people can be achieved by subsidized user rates or by graduated access fees for different institutions, individuals or different sections of communities.

The management software needed to operate the system is complex and its development has taken almost a decade – with much input from teachers, school authorities and students. (In California, teacher support for the programme is so strong that Teachers' and School Supervisors' Unions mobilized $750,000 from their own pension funds to start the first 'Utility' company in that state.) Applications of the system can now be developed further for wider learning and management uses. Other good software already exists for managing the use of integrated technology systems for other purposes – administering hospitals, for example, and maintaining and centralizing patient records. Such management software can be incorporated into a generic system that can make it widely available and so reduce its costs to new users. Equivalent operating management software is now needed for other uses of the combination of technologies – for example, for local government and community management.

The central store and gateway (see Figure 4.1) are owned by a national company. The local storage and processing technology are owned by local Education Utility companies and rented to individual schools. The Utility companies are responsible for installation and maintenance of the equipment and business relations with local educational authorities and other users. The local Utility companies operate under a licensing arrangement with the national company.

The technology

Table 4.1 shows the technology used in the pilot Education Utilities in Arizona, Utah and California to receive, store, process, access and meter digital material supplied by the system. This is 'off-the-shelf' hardware that is already widely available. It is only the software to operate this combination of technologies in their applications for school and community uses that is unique. This software is patented by the Central Education Utility company.

The operating management software makes the list of 'Bundled products provided through lease' shown in Table 4.1 accessible to everyone on the system. All of the hardware listed is provided by the 'Utility' for a monthly rate (similar to a monthly telephone or water rate).

Not all of the items listed in Table 4.1 are essential for the system's operation. A less expensive form of the system could do without the laser printer, for example, or the video capability. The system would still serve a wide variety of learning, management and entertainment functions without live telecommunication. The software stored locally could be updated using new CD disks sent by post. The key principles of the system still apply. As technologies advance, however, and as digital utilities are introduced on a large scale, the costs of the whole set of technologies will be affordable.

COSTS

Establishment costs

Initial capital costs of the technology for a software delivery utility are high. Similarly, the capital cost of hydroelectric dams or power stations for an electricity utility are high – in relation to the income of individual users. When that capital cost is spread over a sufficient number of users, however, the system can be affordable.

There are two important features of software delivery systems, however, which differentiate them from conventional utilities. These are:

Table 4.1 Services and hardware provided by the 'Information and Education Utility'

Applications

MS-DOS Software	Apple Software
Full Motion Video	Interactive Laser Disks
CD-ROM Disks	Live Programs via Satellite
Public Domain Software	Stored Programs via Satellite
Data Bases	Hard Copy Materials

Hardware provided through lease

Satellite Dish	386 Resource Computer
Community Access Server	Modem and Computer Rack
Decoder for Encrypted Data	286 Metering Server
386 Diskless Workstation	386 Workstation
Laser Printer	Video Switcher
Video Storage Unit	CD-ROM Disk Server
Local Area Network	
AG-560 VHS Video Player and Monitor	
Interactive Laser Disk Player	
Uninterruptable Power Supply (UPS)	

Bundled products provided through lease

Administrator Management System
Teacher Management System
Student Management System
Student Grade Books
Daily, Weekly, Monthly Calendars
Individual Note Pad
Computerized Calculator
Word Processor
Electronic Spreadsheet
National Electronic Catalogue Materials
Community User Feature
Global Electronic Mail
Instructional Integrator

The latest technology will add interactive video.

1   Electricity supply utilities have to meet the capital costs of (a) the hydroelectric dam or power station to produce the electricity, and (b) a high voltage network to distribute it. In the case of a software utility, the capital costs of software production are met by the software industry, or by individual agencies commissioning software production, not by the utility. Telecommunication infrastructure – the equivalent to the electricity utility's main power lines – are already in place or their costs are met from other sources.

2   Unlike electricity, water or gas utilities, a software utility is dealing with a saleable product whose use can be sold without the product being depleted. The initial capital and operating costs of the software utility are thus much lower and its profitability higher.

Usage costs

The following example is based on the costs for an individual school programme now operating in the United States. As with other utilities, the costs fall into three categories:

(a) An installation charge – for installing the equipment, the necessary wiring in the schools, and the telecommunication hook-up;

(b) An annual rate – for belonging to the system (currently $2,000 per month);

(c) A usage charge – currently 50 cents for one hour of interactive use of software. (The metering system only records the time that the computer processor is actually operating – not when an item of software is on the screen. Thus, in practice, the actual usage cost is substantially lower than 50 cents per hour of use of the computers.)

The annual charge would cover maintenance costs and costs of updating the technology. For this charge, users receive through the system: word processing, spreadsheets, calendars, E-Mail and public domain software without a user charge.

Let us assume that the school equips four classrooms with thirty terminals (workstations) each. Let us further assume that each terminal is used for two hours per day and for 200 days per year. The annual costs for the school will be $48,000. (Annual rate: 12

months @ 2,000 = 24,000 + usage charge (120 workstations x 400 hours x 50c) = 24,000).

At the same time, the school could hire out access to the system to parents, local authorities, traders and others. The word processing, E-Mail and spreadsheets alone, would be of interest to many community users. They would access the utility by telephone and would provide their own workstations. This would permit children to work at home, and home usage can now be extended to direct distance learning for the parents themselves.

Let us assume that the school rents out access to 100 users at $20 per month. Let us further assume that these users access the system for one hour a day for 300 days in a year. (Good educational software is challenging and fun. There is already evidence of parents increasing their interest in their children's homework – and even of their regular active participation in it! If entertainment software is also accessible through the system, and as more school work is done at home, average usage could quickly exceed an hour per day).

From the 100 users at $20.00 per month the school would receive $24,000 per year. Their one hour's usage for 300 days at 50c per user hour would yield $15,000 per year. Of this, one third would go to the school, one third to the Utility company and one third as a royalty to the software producers.

```
Net income:  Fee to 100 users @ $20/m x 12 months:  24,000
             Usage: 100 x 300 days @ 50c.:                15,000
             Less:    royalty:            5,000
                      Utility Co.         5,000
                      Total Net income:             29,000
```

The total income to the school would therefore be $29,000 per year. In this way, the income to the school would exceed its annual rate charge of $24,000, and could contribute to it's own usage costs. If the external usage increased further, the school could actually make a profit; the hardware and software and it's usage would then cost the school nothing!

Experience has shown that the cost of the system can be further offset by benefits from increasing the efficiency of school operation and management. One school found that by using the processing power of the computer to operate its heating and cooling system, its saving on heating and cooling costs equalled half of its annual rate for belonging to the 'utility'.

This example shows how the utility system removes the obstacle of the capital cost of the hardware and software for the school. Despite the satisfactory mathematics, however, the reader is likely to reject the implied suggestion that a school in the third world can find a monthly rental of $2,000 per month to belong to the system – even if that amount could be recovered from other users. This cost needs to be seen in a different context. It needs to be seen in the light of: (a) the 20 per cent annual reduction in the cost of information referred to at the beginning of the chapter (this will reduce a cost of $100 in 1992 to $32.73 in five years' time and $9.97 in ten years' time); (b) for 'school' read community – in which the school is one of many users, and (c) the principle users of a large digital utility system would be business and industry, government agencies, banks and others, leaving a modest residual for governments to subsidise for educational uses of the system.

The pace of the falling costs and the increases in the power of the technology are indicated in Figure 4.3. These have immediate implications for the profitability of the systems. Greater power increases the speed, ease of operation and breadth of applications

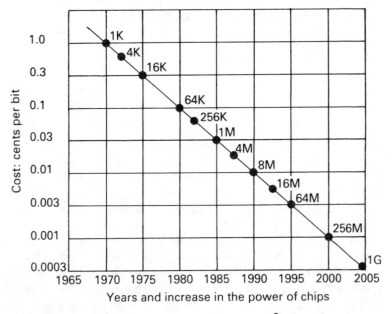

Figure 4.3 The reduction in the cost of processing.[2]

of the technology, while, at the same time, costs and electric power requirements fall. Large scale applications of the technology need to be planned in the context of these trends.

When the principles of the utility's application for the subset of learning which traditionally happens in schools is applied aross its much wider applications in the whole universe of learning, management and entertainment, the system can remove the capital cost obstacles for individual users and institutions in many other fields too. Planning has commenced in a number of countries around the world to apply these principles.

Funding

The example above of the costs for an individual school shows how the system can be affordable to users, and how it removes for them the impediment of the capital costs of having to own hardware and software. However, those capital costs are now transferred to the utilities and still have to be found.

The capital costs of water, electricity and other utilities are either met by governments or raised on the capital markets. The same can apply to new software delivery utilities. In more developed economies, joint leadership from governments, chambers of commerce, and the business community can obtain funding from the capital markets. In less developed countries with modest business and industrial sectors, governments need to take the lead in establishing partnerships with the private sector to develop the new systems. Governments can seek assistance from the international funding bodies to do so.

As digital utilities can be profit-making bodies, they provide new investment opportunities in third world countries for the International Finance Corporation, the local banking community and other agencies funding private sector development. They can also support large scale assembly of low cost terminals and other hardware needed, and development of the local software production capacity that every country will need. Each technical sector of government will want software for its own applications – as well as hardware to link into the new utilities. By providing a means for addressing the communication, learning, management and behaviour change needed in fields of 'new' development priority, the utilities will open up new investment opportunities in these fields too.

Planning for the national 'Community Learning Network' in the United States (described on page 87) is demonstrating how funding from a wide range of sources can be coordinated within a single, large scale informatics programme. In a more limited way, the Teletel programme in France has demonstrated this throughout most of the 1980s.

An element in the funding of the 'utility' programmes in the United States is that a small portion of monthly rate charged to schools for access to the system is paid into an interest earning account in each school's name. The object is that, over a twenty year period, this will grow to a sufficient level to enable the schools to pay off the initial capital investment costs. This concept could have larger application for repayment of loans to countries by international funding bodies and the commercial banking community for the initial capital needed to establish digital utility systems on a large scale.

IMPLICATIONS FOR BUSINESS AND INDUSTRY

All employers have a vested interest in a better product from the education and training systems. In many countries, business is already bearing an unnecessarily heavy cost of training a poorly educated work force – with implications for efficiency and competitiveness. Business therefore needs to support programmes that will improve the product of the education and training systems that serve them. As the pace of development and change accelerate, however, a smaller and smaller proportion of directly job-related skills can be provided by pre-employment education, and more will need to be provided by employers themselves if they are to remain competitive. A recent estimate concluded that those leaving college in the early 1990s will, on average, change jobs four times during their working lifetime. But two of those four jobs have not yet been invented! This has profound implications for the training approaches and programmes that will be needed.

The current annual investment by employers on employee training in the United States has been estimated at 210 billion dollars;[3] that of the US military at 19.6 billion dollars.[4] Of the latter, $2.7 billion, or 13.8 per cent, was spent on training related travel and per diem. A similar proportion of the employer-based training costs would be $29 billion for travel and per diem annually.

In 1991, businesses in the USA with more than 100 employees

spent $43.2 billion on employee training, of which $30.9 billion, or 71 per cent, went on trainers' salaries.[5] The same proportion of the total figure above for all training funded by employers would be $149 billion for trainers' salaries. A software delivery system with two-way, interactive video giving a full motion video link between learners and instructors, could save employers many billions of dollars annually in this field alone.

Against annual figures of this magnitude, and considering the increased timeliness and quality of learning that a software delivery system could achieve, a) the establishment and operational costs of such a system are attainable – even at to-day's prices of the technology, and b) the figures indicate the potential contribution that can be made to the operation of the whole system by its use by business, industry and the military.

IMPLICATIONS FOR THE TELECOMMUNICATION INDUSTRY

A system able to deliver digital material affordably anywhere, any-time has major implications for the telecommunication industry.

Traditionally, telephone companies established and operated telecommunication infrastructure to link increasing numbers of users for voice communication. They have updated their systems as new technologies have become available, and as new uses for their telephones have evolved. But the guiding parameters for the profitable operation of these systems have remained largely unchanged: i.e. (a) establish systems to link users (and, more recently, to link users with central electronic information sources), and (b) charge users for that use on a profitable basis. In practice, users have been those that can afford the luxury of this form of communication. The majority of the people in the world seldom, if ever, use telephones.

The development of telecommunication systems has not been a central item in donor funding in third world countries on the grounds that the private sector can fund the establishment and operation of these potentially profitable enterprises.

The old parameters for the telecommunication industry are changing in four important areas:

1   As mentioned above, telephone companies until now have installed and operated 'bridges' between people and central

information sources. The decentralization of very large data-bases to their intended sites of use and reductions in access costs permit access by people not reached by existing tele-phone systems. This calls for the installation, management, operation and maintenance of an additional and different 'bridge' between (a) centrally available digital information, learning, management, and entertainment materials and local digital storage sites (information and learning centres) and (b) local storage sites and their users.

2   This opens up substantial new market opportunities for tele-communication companies.

3   Digital technologies are now merging old distinctions between telephony and broadcasting. Data compression holds particular potential for social applications of interactive television. Companies able to provide a range of these new services introduce new competition for traditional telephone companies.

4   New perceptions of the communication sector and of the future role of software delivery systems in the social dimension of development will move telecommunication and informatics systems from the periphery to the centre of national socio-economic planning. It will transform the economic justification for investment in telecommunication. In one country recently, investment in a new satellite had been considered too marginal on the basis of conventional uses of telephony. A different perception of the social applications of telecommunication in the future and the additional telecommunication traffic that it will generate has reversed that earlier decision.

The wide ranging benefits to the whole private sector of an infor-matics system for public use creates a new role for chambers of commerce and for industry associations in accelerating understanding and new investment in this field. This is being demonstrated in the leadership by the US Chamber of Commerce described below. This catalytic role of industry-representative organizations in this new field can be replicated worldwide.

JOINT PUBLIC/PRIVATE SECTOR ACTION IN THE USA[6]

The US Chamber of Commerce (USCC) is made up of 3,000 State and local Chambers, 180,000 member corporations and 13,000 trade and professional associations. As indicated above, all have a vested interest in improving the product of the national education and training system. USCC, with support from leading educational and health authorities, the US military, various governmental agencies and a White House Committee, has taken the initiative for building on the Information and Education Utility concept in planning a massive programme to introduce a digital 'utility' system for the United States: 'the Community Learning Network'. This new system will form part of the national AMERICA 2000 programme.

The objective is to establish a national digital information system that can:

> bring integrated, interactive, information technologies to (a) Federal, State, and local governments; (b) communities; (c) educational institutions, and (d) the military for providing low cost, high quality information through shared usage and also be available to business and industry.[7]

At the time of going to press, plans called for establishing software utilities in each of eighty regions in the country. Federal funds were being sought to establish initial operating models at 125 sites.

In December 1991, the Secretary of Defense, Dick Cheyne sent a Directive to the Joint Chiefs of Staff and all the Heads of Departments in the US Military instructing the Assistant Secretary for Force Management and Personnel to implement a Department-wide plan to support the AMERICA 2000 programme. Through its involvement in this programme the US military can mobilize its resources and expertise for peaceful purposes, and adapt some of its most advanced technologies for this objective.

The effect of these advanced technologies, when applied on a large scale, will not be to increase costs, but to increase the capacity and performance of digital utilities at affordable prices. This increase in the capacity of the technology has enormous implications for multi-media applications (the use of voice, pictures and graphics). This in turn has big implications for new approaches to learning and self management worldwide.

In addition to the benefits to member industries of increasing their own efficiency and competitiveness, the Chambers of Commerce in the US also recognize the vast new markets that digital utilities will open up for the information industry, and new investment opportunities for the business and financial communities. Large scale introduction of the systems will call for the production of low cost equipment on a massive scale. In the United States, for example, it is estimated that if 10,000 classrooms are equipped per year to connect to the Community Learning Network, it would take more than 100 years to cover all the classrooms in the country. In India, if a thousand villages per year were equipped with digital Community Learning Centres, it would take 640 years before all villages in the country would be reached. These are not adequate solutions. Much faster programmes are called for.

The plans now being prepared by the USCC include proposals for vocational schools throughout the country to assemble hardware – and obtain income for the schools in the process – and to establish central assembly centres in every State. They also envisage training military personnel to be community leaders in the use of the technology when they return home after finishing their military service. This could be a useful role for surplus military personnel in many countries.

As the planning of this massive programme in the US has progressed, not only has the role of the technology in helping with communities' own self management become clearer, but it has also become apparent that the introduction of the new systems can be used to engineer the restructuring and decentralization of government, as well as to provide a boost to new economic activity and employment.

To sum up so far, an affordable system is now available for linking the different capacities of the whole family of digital technologies to create a new form of public utility. This can harness their combined capacity for addressing the communication, learning, management, local level planning, and other essential human and institutional development functions needed for self-sustaining development. The US Chamber of Commerce has taken a leadership role in the US to bring together business, governmental, military and political leaders to form new partnerships to establish a software delivery system for public use in the United States. This initiative can be replicated widely around the world. Some global implications and key issues are discussed in Part II.

II

A universal telephone service is no longer adequate as a vision for the telecommunication business. A new vision calls for information anytime, anywhere, in any form. To reach towards this vision we must change the process by which we do our work. We must reach beyond services and transport for voice to those for data and video. The process of designing services must focus on users and their needs and capabilities, not on possibilities of network technology.[8]

A COMMUNITY NETWORK

The learning achieved outside schools is much greater than the learning needed in schools. This is extreme in developing countries. Ninety-eight per cent of children in Africa and China do not complete secondary school; there are 500,000,000 illiterate or semi-literate people in India; even in the United States, one child in five has been judged functionally illiterate on leaving high school. Learning is needed among whole adult populations, among the large numbers of early dropouts from school, among children and adults who have never been to school; it is needed for the critical establishment of basic concepts and foundations for learning at pre-school age. What are the roles and potential in these fields of the technologies and concepts outlined in Part 1 and in earlier chapters?

A system able to deal with the delivery, on demand, of information and learning materials for one subset of learning (that which has traditionally taken place in schools) can also assist with a wide range of other forms of learning. We can then think of and approach, the whole spectrum of information transfer and learning differently. The same technology delivers software to assist the administration and management of education systems. It can equally well deliver software for the administration and management of other organizations. The wider the range of users and uses of the same system, the more profitable it can become.

A utility able to deliver information and customized learning materials wherever and whenever needed is of interest to every organization with large educational and training responsibilities. The US military, for example, has 4,600 locations at which training takes place. The US Environmental Protection Agency is responsible for changing the environmental awareness and behaviour of the whole American population. It is assisting with new training programmes across industry to introduce more environmentally friendly technologies and production techniques. Ministries of Health worldwide have, among many other educational responsibilities, a major educational job in the prevention, control and home care of AIDS and in combating increasing drug abuse. Education and training are key objectives of penal correction authorities.

GLOBAL APPLICATIONS

A multi-disciplinary approach to the use of digital systems can overcome the prohibitive costs of their installation for each sector individually. In the United States, $350 billion are spent annually on public education. Of this, approximately 30 per cent is spent on classroom-related costs, of which enough is spent per pupil on learning materials (which can include educational software) to make a software delivery system financially viable in the education sector alone. No other country spends as much on education on a large enough scale to make the same thing possible. In too many countries there are schools that cannot even afford blackboards. Computer instruction in those schools has seemed no closer than the moon. Yet, in a different field, technology has already taken us to the moon!

Generic digital systems can be financially viable if they:

(a) Exploit the potential for shared usage of the same system in its applications for health, agriculture, distance learning, entertainment, local government, banking, training in business and commerce, and so on;

(b) Spread the capital costs of the hardware and software across all of these;

(c) Obtain revenue for the costs of the system from wealthier people and from institutions (government services, business and commerce) to subsidise its use by the poor.

A cross-sectoral approach to the use of the technology makes community information and learning centres possible. These can be entertainment and small business information centres too.

Recovering a charge for these many different uses on a large enough scale could carry the cost of the system so that its use for formal education and by the very poor could be free, or at a purely nominal charge.

Community information and learning centres

The concept of community information and learning centres has been around for some time. There have been attempts to set up small libraries in villages in many countries. Some of these have included videos and video disks from which people can obtain information interactively when they need it. Persistent and unresolved problems have been the cost to governments of maintaining them and the limited number of people in villages in third world countries with the time, reading ability and inclination to use them. New technology can make these centres far more comprehensive and useful than was ever possible using conventional communication media. They can be teleports with fully interactive video systems that provide 'talk-back' television in the community. They can link the private sector (or cooperatives) into operating and maintaining them.

As with libraries, people and organizations will be able to obtain information and instructional, management and entertainment materials from local digital centres as and when they want them. But, unlike libraries, digital information and learning materials can communicate in pictures and sound, as well as in symbols, graphics, script and numbers. They can be in interactive form and can adjust to the learning needs of individual users. They can be updated easily as new material becomes available. Software developed for the blind can 'read' (in sound) from written text. Using touch-screen hardware and appropriate software, literacy and language need no longer be the obstacles to learning that they have been. Also, unlike information in books, digital information and learning materials can be distributed from a community centre to wherever it is convenient in the community to receive them, so making them available to subsets of the communities that have been excluded from community libraries by social barriers.

Agricultural recommendations can be converted into pictorial and graphic form; diagnostic material on human, plant and animal diseases can be available on demand. By linking village learning centres electronically with universities, technical agencies, research stations, hospitals, suppliers and other sources of assistance, the technology can help not only to overcome the remoteness of village life but also to slow – and even reverse – rural to urban migration.

The same technology can help with village management. It can keep individual savings accounts, accessible only through use of the correct thumb print. It has the capacity to transform rural credit. It can help communities to keep inventories on their own natural resources and so improve their management of their environment. It can help them to understand how improvement in environmental husbandry in their own areas can contribute to environmental management needs on a much larger scale. (This is becoming increasingly important in remote mountain communities whose practices are affecting water supply hundreds of miles away. The technology can enable these people to communicate with others down stream.) Software already exists and is in use in all of these fields.

As indicated in preceding chapters, the technology will not replace teachers or field workers in government agriculture, health or other services. It will change their roles from being conveyors of information to being managers of learning processes. It can increase their productivity and raise their status. It can be used to upgrade them and to keep them continually informed of new developments.

Examples of relevant experience

A few examples indicate both the wide range of experience that already exists and the confines of single-sector approaches. These and a great many other programmes can now be built upon to utilize the generic potential of the technology multi-sectorally.

The President of Costa Rica enlisted IBM's assistance to introduce computer-based learning in schools. Now more than 50 per cent of school children in Costa Rica have access to varying amounts of computer-based instruction. These schools have been double streamed to permit access by the children to the limited numbers of computers. The status of the schools and of the teachers in the communities have been enhanced. Parents come to the schools in the evening to benefit from the instruction. However, learning by the parents is confined to the limited range of software available in each school for literacy, maths and science. They benefit from these but their individual priority learning requirements might be book-keeping, repair of an irrigation pump, a health need and so on. The priority learning requirements of the adults have been subordinated to the 'computers in schools' approach. Now, by increasing local memory and processing power and by introducing the 'utility' concept, the use of the schools' computers in Costa Rica can serve a much broader learning function. They can respond to the individual learning priorities of a wide range of users and can be used for local management, planning and entertainment purposes as well.

The same thing can be applied to successful but narrow uses of the technology in other fields.

1   A programme in this new field in India (described below) grew out of an initiative by the Ministry of Rural Development which linked computers at village level to the national network for data gathering for rural planning purposes.
2   A rural banking initiative in Malaysia could provide a base on which to build a rural informatics programme.
3   In Denmark, there is a well established computer network linking agricultural cooperatives which could be built upon.
4   In South Africa, planning has already commenced for a utility system that will focus on the national priority of 'social advancement'. This calls for accelerated improvement of a wide range of social services for the disadvantaged sections of the population.
5   In Czechoslovakia, an initiative by the tax authorities to improve tax collection has led to a digital system for broader local government purposes. This could be developed further into a public utility.
6   In the UK, the 'Tele-Cottage' programme has linked homes in remote parts of Scotland with companies in urban centres. The latter send accounting, design and editing work electronically to the rural dwellers, who do the work required and return the finished product the same way.
7   Major airlines in the United States send used ticket data to several islands in the Caribbean where contracted workers undertake the reconciliation work and return the results by fax and electronic mail. The airlines benefit from the lower labour costs in the islands and the islands benefit from the employment created.
8   In France, the Teletel programme could be developed further with the decentralization of greater memory and processing power.

9   In several countries, cable television companies are in a
     position to lead the way by installing co-axial cables (capable
     of handling video and other digital communication in two
     directions). From being just suppliers of entertainment they
     could take advantage of the much wider applications of the
     same technologies.

Another example illustrates the need in a different way. A number of
European countries contributed to the 'EUROSTEP' programme.
Through this initiative, space on the most advanced European
satellite was made freely available for education purposes for a five
year period. Leading educational institutions and other important
sources of digital learning materials all participated.

   Thus, there were, at one end, pre-eminent educational
institutions keen to make instruction and instructional materials
available and, at the other, educational institutions needing this
input; in between was a sophisticated communication channel.
However, an essential element was missing. Relatively few schools
and universities had the equipment to use the digital material
being made freely available and many lacked access to the satellite.
The 'utility' concept demonstrated by the 'Information and
Education Utility' programme in the United States would have
provided the missing ingredient. By adding this, in order to receive
and administer digital material, and by supplying the necessary
equipment, the 'bridge' would have been complete. Without this
ingredient, it fell far short of its funders' good intentions.

The initiative in India

Emphasis on technology development in India over the past
twenty years has produced great benefits to business, industry and
public sector management. All major cities are linked by an
advanced computer network. This now extends to 460 districts.
Until recently, however, most of the 700 million rural people in
India had had little or no direct benefit from these advances. A
great many small, isolated programmes in India are demonstrating
the potential of digital technologies at village level. Several
governmental programmes have also extended the national
network to village or block (municipal) level for specific purposes,
such as rural development planning, literacy, water resource
monitoring and control and health matters.

In November 1990, the Government of India initiated a joint public/private sector programme to introduce an 'Informatics System for Community Use' – thus making India the first country to do this. India's huge resource of trained software producers (currently estimated at 160,000 in India and about 60,000 abroad) can design software based on the villagers' perceptions of their needs. Most of this software will not require literacy; it will make use of graphics, symbols and sound – making it easier to adapt for use in other third world countries. This could become a significant export product for India. (India exported software in conventional fields worth $US100 million in 1990.)

Software industry leaders in India saw the potential market for their products in the country's 640,000 villages if a system to reach those villages could be devised. They led an initiative to apply the 'utility' concept developed in the USA to the Indian rural population. They saw that this would be economically feasible only if the multi-functional uses of the technology were approached from the outset. This required the support of all of the larger technical agencies of government, the Electronics Department and the central planning authorities.

An 'Informatics System for Community Use' is still at an initial stage of development in India but virtually all of the present-day hardware needed is already in production in the country. The experience from the wide range of successful but fragmented uses of the technology at village level in the country can now be combined and replicated through distribution of the software by means of a generic system. It will provide the proof of the potential and economic feasibility of such a system. (With the falling costs of the technology shown in Figure 4.3 on page 82, the financial viability of an informatics system will be much greater by the time that a system is in place at community level on a large scale in India.)

Indian authorities believe that many people in typical, moderately sized villages can pay small amounts for a range of uses of the system and that a variety of governmental and other agencies, such as banks, traders and NGOs would use it too. Together these could make the system financially viable. Its use could then be made free of charge for formal education and either free or at reduced rates for poorer segments of the communities. This could provide a model for third world countries – and for others.

IMPLEMENTATION

Digital utilities for public use are new. The institutional structures do not yet exist to which these new systems can belong. None has a mandate for their planning, establishment and funding.

All countries can now develop their information industries and the social applications of digital systems. (The smallest and poorest countries will have to do this in cooperation with their wealthier neighbours.) The countries best able to lead new initiatives are those with more developed information economies and a high priority on social programmes. To move into this new field, however, all countries need to establish a point of responsibility and expertise for initiating the new planning and investment programmes needed. In the United States, Jack Taub with his remarkable charisma, took on this responsibility himself. Now the Chambers of Commerce, the US military and many government agencies are supporting his initiative. In India it was the software industry that led a joint public/private sector initiative to create this focus of responsibility. In South Africa a consortium of electronic industries has taken on this role. In Malaysia, an initiative by the banking industry may prove to be the catalyst for a 'utility' programme.

Figure 4.4 shows the essential functions of the initiating body needed to lead the introduction of the new utilities, and relationships between this new entity and existing organizations. These new bodies must have access to, and support from, national planners, and the participation of their countries' leading authorities in technology. They need to have contact with, and be responsive to the needs of, major potential user groups – such as education, health, local government, banking, etc. The initiating bodies need to be representative of both the hardware (delivery) and software (content) industries. These industries will be the greatest financial beneficiaries from the new flow of funds to develop the communication sector. They should provide leadership in establishing the initiating bodies.

In developing countries these new bodies need to participate, with governments, in a new dialogue with (a) the major donor agencies, (b) funders of private sector development – (such as the International Finance Corporation) and (c) foreign hardware and software industries that can become partners in private sector consortia. The new bodies need to provide leadership in

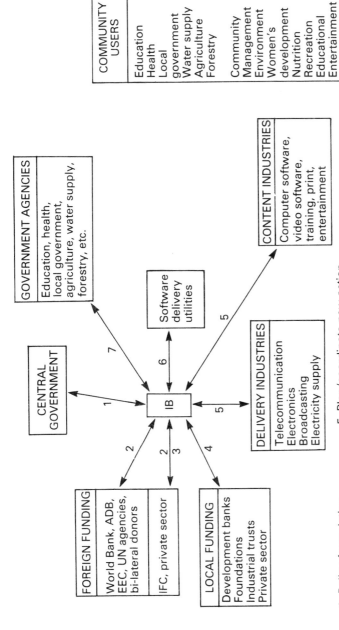

COMMUNITY USERS

Education
Health
Local government
Water supply
Agriculture
Forestry

Community Management
Environment
Women's development
Nutrition
Recreation
Educational Entertainment

GOVERNMENT AGENCIES

Education, health, local government, agriculture, water supply, forestry, etc.

CENTRAL GOVERNMENT

FOREIGN FUNDING

World Bank, ADB, EEC, UN agencies, bi-lateral donors

IFC, private sector

LOCAL FUNDING

Development banks
Foundations
Industrial trusts
Private sector

IB

Software delivery utilities

DELIVERY INDUSTRIES

Telecommunication
Electronics
Broadcasting
Electricity supply

CONTENT INDUSTRIES

Computer software, video software, training, print, entertainment

1. Policy formulation
2. Influence foreign investment
3. Seek foreign partners
4. Obtain local funding
5. Plan/coordinate new action
6. Initiate new utilities
7. Dialogue with major user agencies

Figure 4.4 Functions of the initiating body.

demonstrating the new systems in their own countries, defining the nature of the new utilities, and establishing the utilities and the institutional structures needed for their implementation so that these can become new items on the macro-economic planning agenda.

The consortium in South Africa referred to above has deliberately kept numbers of participants small to begin with to facilitate starting a new programme quickly. Once established, they intend to allow a broad spectrum of information industries to participate in the consortium to develop a national programme. This model is replicable in many countries.

NEW INVESTMENT OPPORTUNITIES

Digital utilities can be profitable. This provides new investment opportunities in third world countries for National Development Banks, the International Finance Corporation, the business community and other agencies supporting private sector development. Large scale assembly of low cost terminals and other necessary hardware, and support for software producers will create new employment opportunities and a boost for countries' economies.

Much funding for third world development has flowed from governments of richer countries and multilateral donor agencies to governments of poorer countries, and through their technical agencies to achieve the respective development purposes of those agencies – education, health, agriculture, etc. As indicated in earlier chapters, a feature of development aid worldwide is that government bureaucracies have expanded to handle new programmes; a progressively larger proportion of new funding has gone to maintaining the bureaucracies, and a progressively smaller proportion of each new investment has reached the intended beneficiaries. This traditional funding channel is shown in Figure 4.5.

The advent of digital utilities provides new investment opportunities for governments, donor agencies, the information industry and private capital sources. It provides new routes through which development funds can flow, and will develop private sector capability to support social advancement. This alternative is also shown in Figure 4.5. In addition, each technical sector of government will want software for its own applications –

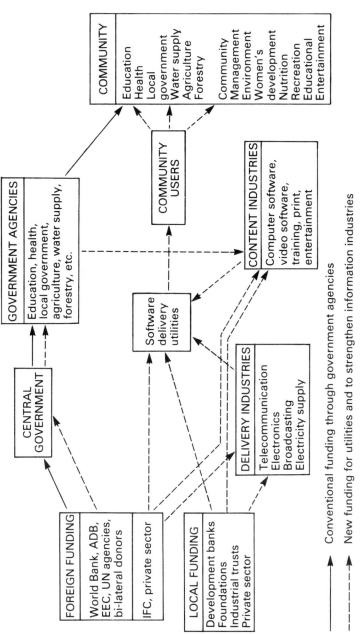

Figure 4.5 Funding for a digital utility for public use.

COMMUNITY

Education
Health
Local government
Water supply
Agriculture
Forestry

Community Management
Environment
Women's development
Nutrition
Recreation
Educational
Entertainment

GOVERNMENT AGENCIES

Education, health, local government, agriculture, water supply, forestry, etc.

COMMUNITY USERS

CONTENT INDUSTRIES

Computer software, video software, training, print, entertainment

CENTRAL GOVERNMENT

Software delivery utilities

DELIVERY INDUSTRIES

Telecommunication
Electronics
Broadcasting
Electricity supply

FOREIGN FUNDING

World Bank, ADB, EEC, UN agencies, bi-lateral donors

IFC, private sector

LOCAL FUNDING

Development banks
Foundations
Industrial trusts
Private sector

⟶ Conventional funding through government agencies

⟶ ⟶ New funding for utilities and to strengthen information industries as well as hardware to link into the new utilities. Donor agencies that finance governmental development programmes in third world countries can help to fund this. The technology will also open up new investment opportunities in fields of 'new priority' in development.

A primary role of the initiating bodies referred to above and shown in Figure 4.4 is to create the understandings, and help to formulate the policies and strategies, that are needed to change the flow of funds from the traditional routes to the routes needed to develop countries' information industries and new utilities.

MAJOR OBSTACLES

Obvious obstacles to the rapid development of informatics systems for public use worldwide and particularly in third world countries, include cost; available hardware and software; electricity supplies; and maintenance. Other important issues will be policies; standards; security of software and intellectual property rights; and the ownership of utility systems. The manpower and skills required will be vital to all of these.

A further problem, in both developed and less developed countries alike, is that digital utilities are fundamentally new. They lack an established track record and there is little public awareness to support their public funding. Whole books have been written on most of these subjects. Some key considerations in each of them are addressed in the following sections.

Costs and cost recovery

Costs of a totally new public utility are substantial. The long term programme to cover the whole of the United States, reaching every school and community, has an initial price tag of $100 billion. (This is a modest amount in relation to the cost of establishing a new water or electricity utility on the same scale.) If the software utilities can be a profitable investment; if industry and the capital markets can provide much of the funds needed, and if creation of the 'utilities' generates large scale new employment, that $100 billion investment will have a very different effect on stimulating economic activity and a far greater developmental role than an equivalent investment in conventional social services.

No developing country can envisage a country-wide programme

reaching to remote and dispersed communities in the short term. Each one can identify particular areas, however, with high population density and existing telecommunication infrastructure in which to initiate viable programmes. Countries can use these selected areas to build expertise, experience and stocks of software. Meanwhile, technologies and miniaturization will advance and costs will diminish.

Two key elements of cost recovery are the metering of the use of software and the local institutional capacity to supervise accounts and to pursue payments. In communities in developed countries, many of the accounts (and the utilities' revenue) will be from individual families. Cost recovery will be a major logistical exercise. In developing countries for the foreseeable future, particularly in rural areas, most usage will be by institutions, including communities, with most of the revenue from the former. Governments will subsidize the social development uses of software – for distance learning, agriculture, health, formal education, community management and other purposes; banks will be able to recover the cost of banking software through individuals' accounts and other services can do the same. Advertisers can provide another source of revenue for the utility companies. These can all simplify cost recovery for the utility authorities.

In South Africa, a rural telephone programme is demonstrating how villagers can be given access to telephones by using magnetic telephone cards. The cost of each call is automatically recorded on the card at the end of the call and the remaining face value is shown on the card. People have individual code numbers for security of their cards. The cards can be made available at subsidized rates to different individual categories of users. (The intention of the programme was to encourage and facilitate the use of telephones by rural people. Experience so far is that many of the cards are bought by people in the cities who send them to their relatives and friends in rural areas to help them to communicate with the people in the cities.)

The same principle can be applied to the use of a multi-functional informatics system at community level. Cards can be coded for different categories of use and users and subsidized by governments – or others – as desired.

Within the time in which widespread establishment of digital utility systems can be envisaged realistically, and assuming that a substantial portion of the investment needed comes from the private sector, the capital costs are feasible. Meanwhile, the cost for all countries of not realizing the potential of digital technologies is ruinous. Already the world's financial and commodity markets and much of its international trade are dependent on digital communication technology and computers. Smaller and poorer developing countries see theirselves being relegated even more than before to spectator status in these fields unless they have the skills and equipment they need. The option facing governments if they do not exploit the social applications of informatics is: (a) to continue to increase their investment in inefficient and restrictive traditional approaches and (b) to expand those approaches to address 'new' priorities in development which they have excluded until now. The costs of such an option are prohibitive.

The hardware

A great deal is possible with the hardware available today. The technology shown in Table 4.1 on page 79 is already manufactured in countries with more advanced information economies and is available in all countries except those with the smallest markets. Although the highly sophisticated technology needed to produce computer chips will remain in the most advanced countries, most other countries can either produce or develop the capacity to produce all but a few specialized parts of the hardware needed. Assembly of the hardware is a far less sophisticated affair and all countries can develop local capacity to do this. In all but the smallest countries, the scale of the demand for new hardware that the utilities will create will justify development of local assembly capabilities and will create new employment opportunities and economic activity at the same time.

Poorer third world countries would do well not to spurn the rapidly growing secondhand market in hardware. As more advanced technologies and more demanding applications are appearing, large organizations in the more advanced economies are replacing existing equipment in wholesale fashion. Thus, little-used equipment is now regularly entering the secondhand market at a small fraction of the original purchase price. The largest secondhand dealer in the United States has over 50,000 units in stock – most of which could be linked into a software delivery system.

Looking only a short way into the future, the reduction in the cost of new technologies and the potential benefits of interactive video and multi-media interfaces will warrant an upgrading of the technology for delivery systems. This will be needed particularly for uses of multi-media in community information, learning, management and entertainment centres. However, a feature of the advancing technology is that the more sophisticated the technology becomes the more it can do, and so highly developed technologies will still be able to communicate with existing hardware. A little further down the road, next generation hardware will be so inexpensive that it will be feasible to replace the hardware generally available today. Countries with less developed information economies, which lack the skilled manpower to initiate major programmes in this new field immediately, will benefit by entering the field a few years hence and beginning with more advanced hardware.

Electricity

A common response to the idea of computers in villages in third world countries is: 'Impossible! There's no electricity in villages.'

Rural electrification schemes have connected a surprising number of villages in third world countries to mains power supplies (though the power supply may be erratic). In irrigated areas, power to operate tube wells has often been extended for village use. In a great many villages, including some in very remote locations, clinics have fridges operated by solar power. These have been installed by international immunization programmes. The solar panels have proved remarkably reliable. In Somalia, after five years in operation, the most serious problem with the panels was reported to be teaching the villagers to dust them after sand storms without scratching their surface. Almost all third world countries are in the tropics and sub-tropics. Strong solar energy is available to all of them throughout the year.

Non-technical people typically think of a computer needing 240 or 110 volts (depending on the country in which they live). This is the voltage at which they receive electricity from their power supply company. It is not the voltage that their computers need. Most computers operate on 12 volts, while printers may need 20 volts. With one additional battery, the solar panels already installed in rural clinics to operate fridges can also operate computers.

The lack of generally available and reliable electricity in many villages appears to be a problem. To the solar power industry, struggling to be recognized as an important resource in most countries, this situation is an opportunity.

Maintenance

A rural telephone system to reach remote mountain villages in western Taiwan uses small computer operated satellite receivers run by solar energy. The computers are programmed for their own fault diagnosis. The electronics of the computers are designed on three colour-coded boards. The fault diagnosis entails the computer simply indicating which coloured board contains a problem. Maintenance consists of sliding out the faulty board and replacing it with a new one. Training local people to be proficient in the simple maintenance procedures takes only a few hours. The same principle can be applied to the design and maintenance of the digital 'utility' technology.

Concerns have been voiced over the care that rural or urban communities will take of digital utility equipment. Experience generally in third world countries is that computers in villages have been treated with respect and pride. They are symbols of development and modernity. While they provide valued services, they are likely to be cared for. Moreover, if communities have to enter into formal agreements with utility companies and pay a monthly rate for the equipment, then (a) they are not so likely to associate the equipment with unpopular governments and so regard it with disrespect, and (b) the equipment can be withdrawn if it is not looked after – to the disadvantage of the whole community.

Awareness and leadership

Digital software delivery systems and community information and learning centres are new. They do not belong to any one of the existing disciplines or sectors in which governments and donor agencies are organized. Thus, governments lack budgets and policies in this field. The role and mandate of middle managers in any existing organization do not extend to initiating a multi-sectoral programme in digital technology applications. Leadership for new initiatives in this field, therefore, needs to come from the highest levels of government, donor agencies and the private sector. These leaders should recognize that the four key elements of the leadership now needed are:

(a) To create the conceptual, intellectual understanding of this new phenomenon;
(b) To obtain and allocate funds to demonstrate and develop the technology;
(c) To initiate new planning processes for cross-sectoral approaches to the communication sector;
(d) To equip their organizations with appropriate staff and policies to operate in the new context that the technology and concepts create.

It is significant that the first Education Utility programmes in the USA are in Arizona and Utah – neither in the centres of technology development nor in the wealthiest states. The reason is principally that in these smaller states it has been easier to gather together key leaders and to obtain their understanding, support and commitment. Similarly, in the UK, it will be easier to obtain the critical mass of support for digital utilities for public use in Scotland and Wales than in England.

Smaller developing countries have an advantage in this respect. In those countries, it will be much easier to bring together key players and decision makers in government, industry, business, academia and NGOs for new national initiatives.

OVERCOMING RESISTANCE

A brief description is relevant here of the process that took place in India to gain multi-disciplinary support for a programme to establish 'an informatics system for community use'. It was necessary to overcome the initial (and natural) resistance of managers in each technical sector who had little or no background in information technology. The idea of a major role for a high technology system in rural India was new. It seemed to have little place in the rural poverty of India.

At separate meetings with senior officials from each technical sector and subsector, the managers were asked about any interesting examples that they knew of in their sectors of uses of interactive technologies. In every case, the officials described innovative programmes in which the technology was being used successfully at village level. This led on to discussions of comparable experiences in other countries, all of which demonstrated the potential of the technologies in various applications.

When asked whether the successes in their individual sectors had spread and what was being done to replicate the experience, the responses were uniform. The cost of the equipment and its maintenance implications were too great to allow any one sector to expand its successes widely.

When the concept of a generic delivery system was described – through which each sector could spread its successes without a large capital outlay and could introduce successful applications from elsewhere – every agency agreed to participate in a new national initiative. The Government of India established a joint public/private sector body, with representation from the information industries and business community, to lead the development of 'an informatics system for community use'. A similar approach is needed in other countries (and development agencies) to create a cross-sectoral environment of understanding and support for a generic system.

Pilot trials and demonstrations of the technology in India – as in other countries – can build on existing initiatives where computers are already in use at local levels for narrow, single-sector purposes. This can be done by adding to the many successful, single-sector initiatives in different parts of the world, some of which were referred to above.

A more substantial obstacle than any of the above and one to which governments need to give high priority, is software – and all that relates to it.

Software

In Chapter 2, the infrastructure of the communication sector was described as its skeleton and information and communication materials as its flesh. Likewise, digital utilities form the skeleton of a new communication system but the flesh of that system is the software it can deliver.

Software is already in use in third world countries for a wide range of developmental activities. Most of it is scattered among numerous independent, single-discipline programmes. There is a surprising amount already in use at village level. Already there is wasteful duplication of effort in software production both within and across countries for lack of coordinating bodies in this new field.

The science of producing good instructional software is advancing rapidly. The increasing capacity of the technology enables the software to be more and more user-friendly. In the United States, there are over 17,000 items of educational software approved for use in the public school system. The science of instructional software design has advanced to the point where only about 10 per cent of this material is up to the standards now demanded. A large body of software exists internationally in the health sector; in the UK there are 55 companies now producing agricultural software, and so on. Experience is showing, however, that there are strong cultural overtones in the acceptance of instructional software. This is not limited to developing countries. In the UK, for example, there is evidence of resistance to American learning materials. But where the same materials have been translated into a British context they have been accepted. In widely differing cultures, of course, the misfit and resistance are far greater.

Western dominance

A well grounded fear is that the information revolution will provide further opportunity for the developed countries to dominate and to impose their views of the world on less developed countries. In contrast, the nature of digital utilities can provide a vehicle for reducing the dominance of the 'north' over the 'south'.

Experience shows that where people have to pay to use information and learning materials, they will do so only if the materials meet one of three criteria:

(a) The materials have to be useful, i.e. in terms of the perceptions of the users;
(b) They have to be entertaining, or
(c) The cost is disguised.

The viability of digital utilities depends on their use. It therefore depends on the software available being acceptable to their users. This calls for software producers to focus on assessing software needs from the point of view of users at village level and to produce software in the context of those cultures. At village level, most people are not seeking information on central government budgets, development policies or international relations. They want information to answer specific, usually simple, questions concerning immediate problems in their daily lives. They will pay small amounts to obtain that information. The utilities offer the opportunity of tailoring information for development to the needs and contexts of the 'south'.

All countries need to build up their software production capacity, either to produce their own software or to be able to adapt foreign material. The costs and technology involved in computer manufacture exclude most countries from being major players in this field. The same does not apply to software design.

While the communication process has had a low profile and priority in third world development, so too has the development of the capability to produce information and entertainment. This has left those countries open to low cost, low quality material from outside – in printed, filmed, taped or dramatized forms.

Different perceptions of information, of the communication and learning process and of the development of people will give new priority to the importance of rejecting poor quality foreign material, to maintaining cultural values and heritage and to using interactive technologies in so doing.

Standards and quality control

The whole question of standards and compatibility of hardware and software will become critical to the rate of development of generic systems for public use. Software producers will only make software available to utilities if they are secure. Security is central to the private sector's interest and investment in the utilities. This calls for joint action by governments, the industry and international bodies. It needs to be addressed at an early stage or else a confusion of standards will hamper the development of digital delivery systems.

Based on performance of the digital technology industry to date, it may seem unrealistic to expect agreements on standards. The large scale social applications of the technology, however, comprise a very different market from the high value markets in commerce, industry and finance for which the technology has been developed to date. In that market, individual industries and companies have sponsored customized systems for their own uses.

It has been possible to operate in this market without uniform standards and governments have played little part in establishing standards.

This approach will not be possible in the social sector where very large numbers of users and small margins will be the norm. A lack of standards will be too costly and inefficient for the digital utilities to be viable – particularly in poorer countries where margins will be smallest. The vast potential market in the public uses of informatics systems is accessible only if appropriate standards are established. The nature of the market will dictate the standards that it requires. It will be to the benefit of all parties to agree on the necessary standards. Governments will have a strong interest in the viability of software delivery systems which link the private sector into the delivery of public services, so they will play a larger part in establishing standards than they have needed to until now.

An obvious danger of a software delivery system is that it could quickly become flooded with poor quality software. The Education Utility programme in the United States has an in-built 'cleaning process'. At the end of each month a record can be produced of the use of every item of software in the system. Software which is not used over a given period can be dropped from the system. A screening system for new software is needed too. In the United States, the EPIE centres,[9] first established under the Academy of Sciences, have responsibility for approving all software for the public school system. Something similar will be needed in other countries as an essential item in a multi-disciplinary approach to establishing digital utilities. An equivalent function will be needed by the technical sectors and other user agencies to vet software in their respective fields.

Misuse

Some fear that electronic information and learning systems will be misused for political and other purposes. This would be possible. However, an argument for not investing in those systems on these grounds is equivalent to arguing against building roads on the grounds that armies can drive tanks down them. In both cases, the benefits far outweigh the negative potential – and it is the job of responsible government to establish safeguards against the latter.

Skilled workforce

The pace of realizing all of the technical, physical and financial possibilities of the technology and its applications outlined above will be confined by countries' stocks of skilled workers to implement new programmes. This calls for governments and donor agencies to anticipate the new era. Highest priority in almost every country will need to be given to developing the skills and programmes to produce the skilled workforce required.

Most of the skills, resources and instructional capability in these new fields are to be found in the information industry, not in traditional educational institutions. Governments can establish joint ventures with the private sector to draw upon those resources – as well as orienting existing educational systems to broaden their programmes to provide the basic skills and understandings needed in this field.

WHAT NEXT?

Incredible new reductions in size, cost and speed of digital equipment will soon leapfrog the technologies that have made the Education Utility and other educational and management applications possible. For example, the technology already exists to make the electronics of a conventional PC smaller than a matchbox, costing less than $US10. Within a year from now, 80 megabyte interactive memories will be on the market that will be about the size of a standard credit card (and 1 centimetre thick). These reductions in size are accompanied by equivalent reductions in power requirements. A typical lap-top computer currently has a battery life of only a few hours. A notepad computer is about to appear on the market which will run continuously for two days on a 1.5 volt rechargeable battery.

An indication of the continuing reduction in costs and increases in power of the technology is indicated in Figure 4.3 on page 82. Translating Figure 4.3 into more physical terms:

By 1986, a million transistors could be put on a quarter-inch square silicon wafer. By 1990, Megabit Random Access Memory (RAM) had arrived. Technology was available to put four million transistors on the same sized wafer. Quarter micron chips carrying tens of millions of transistors will be commonplace by 1994. Parallel development of gallium arsenide technology, optical chips and ballistic transistor technology will add their potentials. In a ballistic transistor, for example, the electrons move so fast that they can switch at 10 Femto seconds (1 Femto second = 1 quadrillion of a second).

Work has begun to produce a very high speed (200 MIPS), cordless computer terminals (like a cordless telephone) weighing less than five pounds. Produced in large numbers, their cost could be less than $US1,000. This would form the primary 'next generation' terminal for widespread introduction in the United States in association with the AMERICA 2000 programme.

These technologies will all increase the portability of information and interactive learning materials. Multiple applications of these technologies in upgrading government field advisory services everywhere and in their use by the services and by remote communities have yet to be explored. They will not do away with the Community Information and Learning Centres referred to earlier in this chapter but will make them more affordable. They will extend the principle and applications of decentralized memory and processing power. Hundreds of millions of people live in concentrated communities in irrigated areas. Here, Community Learning Centres can serve large numbers of people. But in drier areas and in areas of larger agricultural holdings, rural households are scattered and communication with them is more difficult and expensive. In these situations, Community Centres have limited applications. Substantial, but inexpensive, processing power and updatable interactive memories can extend the principle of information/ learning centres to small, satellite subcentres. They can help to overcome the present difficulty of communicating with scattered populations. They have a major role in organized distance learning and in helping communities to manage their own affairs.

Just for the rich?

One's first reaction may well be that the technology's costs and sophistication will exclude the poor and further benefit the better off. In fact, the outcome may be very different. An electronic delivery system can, for the first time in history, make the same information, knowledge, advice and high quality instructional materials accessible to rich and poor alike and can tailor information and instructional materials to the needs and perceptions of the poor and the uneducated.

Most communication and information transfer for development to date has taken place in the context of 'We know; they don't. Send it to them!'

This was partly inevitable when communication systems were mostly one-way and most development information was technical. Software delivery systems will be viable only if the material that they supply is useful to the receivers and if the systems are used by a large number of people.

Various programmes in different parts of the world have shown how the technology can help communities in planning to include all of their members, without confronting the social standing of the more advantaged. The technology has the capacity to help people – all people! It permits mass personalization of information regardless of location, level of education, social background or economic status. The challenge before us is to realize the technology's potential.

Not a panacea

Digital technology is not a panacea or great elixir. It is not a technological salvation for development. Informatics systems for public use will not come about overnight – though we may all be surprised by how soon they will be introduced in a great many countries. The technology is a tool of extraordinary potential which, as its development advances, is becoming better and better able to handle software that uneducated people can use. New concepts that help us to see the identity of the social dimension of development in its own right, together with electronic delivery systems and better use of conventional communication systems, will enable development to move beyond the point that it has reached.

CONCLUSION

Decentralized, digital software delivery systems go beyond anything that has existed until now. They introduce a tool for revolutionizing traditional approaches to formal education and governments' advisory services; for helping to increase the efficiency of government bureaucracies; for the decentralization of governance; for distance education; for entertainment and for the empowerment of people and communities. They also provide a means of linking the private sector into the delivery of public services on a large scale for the first time. This opens up a vast market for the information industry and calls for a review of the role of telecommunication in development. Generic systems can benefit all existing technical sectors but do not 'belong' within any one of them. New leadership is called for at the highest levels of governments, donor agencies, academia, Foundations and the information industry, in order to realize the potential of digital utility systems. These agencies need to equip themselves both technically and with new policies and strategies for introducing digital utilities and developing their applications.

Digital utilities create new markets for the information industry worldwide, and new investment opportunities for the international donor community in third world countries. A new location of responsibility must be created in every country, however, to lead joint public/private sector action in this new field. Models in the United States, India and South Africa are already showing how this can be done.

Obstacles to the introduction of the new utilities are formidable. The greatest obstacles, however, are not in technical or financial fields. They lie in (a) creating the necessary understanding among policy makers, planners and funding agencies worldwide of the nature of this new phenomenon, and (b) overcoming natural pressures to maintain the status quo and reluctance to embark into a new unknown field.

Chapter 2 outlined the nature of the communication sector; Chapter 3 showed why this sector has been neglected in conventional development approaches. The digital technologies and digital utility systems described in this chapter permit development to move beyond the confines of the existing organizational structures and current productivity-centred approaches to address the central imperative of developing people, communities and institutions. We can re-think development approaches for achieving social objectives.

If we can now re-think development approaches for communication and social development, can we re-think conventional wisdom in other fields too? Possibilities that emerge when we allow ourselves to question accepted theory and practice in other important fields are discussed in the next chapter.

Chapter 5

Implications and applications

> We need to change our own view point if we are to best understand some of the important issues that will face us during the 1990s.[1]

The question of how to re-cut the 'development cake' was posed at the end of Chapter 1. Should we: (a) reduce the slice for each existing sector to release funds for the new components? or (b) is there an alternative?

In the 1980s, governments and major donor agencies chose option (a), but gave priority to 'productive' sectors at the expense of the social sectors. As evidence of the insufficiency of this option grew towards the end of the decade, there was new concern, effort and investment to address social objectives of development – but without new tools to do so. New perceptions of the communication sector in development, and the new tool that a generic, digital utility system provides for helping to achieve a wide range of human development functions change the context within which we can now approach the social dimension of development. An alternative now exists.

It is reasonable for readers to ask: 'Is it possible to "discover" a new sector – the communication sector – after so much effort, thought, money and good intention has been devoted to development already?' The answer is 'Yes!' – for the reasons outlined in Chapter 3.

We can go further. If we now 'find' a sector which was not generally seen to exist before, and if, previously, we equated the sum of the activities of the conventional sectors with 'development' and now find that these equal only part of development, could there be something fundamentally amiss with the thinking on which those earlier perceptions was based? Is it possible that the familiar sectors do not have the validity that we have assumed?

This chapter shows that the answer to these questions too is 'Yes'. It outlines some of the new opportunities that open up when we accept and face these conclusions.

THE VALIDITY OF CONVENTIONAL DISCIPLINES

Most development to date has been conceived and planned within the confines and mandates of individual disciplines and sectors. We saw in Chapter 3 how each sector has been staffed by professionals who were programmed by their training to produce solutions in their respective professional fields. We have had little need or incentive to question the validity of those disciplines and sectors. Now the confines of the artificial boundaries of the traditional disciplines are becoming more and more apparent. We need to break out of those confines. New possibilities and opportunities open up when we do so.

The following examples from education, agriculture, health, nutrition, forestry, community mobilization, women's development, water and environment show how changes are occurring in what these areas have been perceived to be. This has significant implications for what we perceive 'development' itself to be and for how we cut the development 'cake' in the future.

Education

In Chapters 2 and 4, we saw how new electronic systems will revolutionize formal education and make it possible to advance from existing, standardized approaches of formal education to customized education. The same digital system can assist with the education of adults and with distance learning. It can handle entertainment too, so traditional barriers between 'education' and 'entertainment' can be realigned. We can improve upon orthodox approaches and can alter the location, time and manner in which learning takes place. This will change traditional perceptions of what 'education' is.

There is another aspect. Research is showing the very strong influence that home background can have on children's performance in school. Findings vary from home background contributing an average of about 40 per cent to student achievement in the USA to approximately 60 per cent in the UK and Germany and even more in Scandinavia. This compares with figures of about 10–20 per cent in Eastern Asian countries and less that 5 per cent in Africa.

To date, almost all investment in education in third world countries has been equated with school and university systems and has focused on children and adolescents – this being the mandate and experience of most educators. If home background and parents' knowledge and level of education can contribute more than 60 per cent to children's achievement in school, it raises the question: how much of a country's investment for 'education' should go to the education of parents and how much to children? This question is particularly pertinent in those third world countries which show the lowest contribution of home background to school performance and where the very survival of many children depends on changes in knowledge and practices on the part of their parents. The conventional profile of investment in countries' education can and must change. A system that can provide interactive learning materials to children and adults alike can help in achieving this change.

Agriculture

From antiquity, agricultural practices changed slowly. Improvements came about in a pioneering process. The pace of change accelerated in the eighteenth century in Europe and then in North America and elsewhere as scientific thought and discoveries began to be applied to agricultural husbandry. Agriculture moved from a 'pioneering' stage to a 'production' stage. This gained momentum with new knowledge of genetics, plant and animal breeding and nutrition, soil science and other technical advances. The 'production' stage progressed until the Second World War called for large scale intensification of production. Farm management principles were developed and applied in earnest; maximizing economic returns became a primary objective. Agriculture moved from a 'production' stage to an emphasis on 'productivity'.

Short term farm management models calling for high input/output approaches could not take account of the longer term damaging effects of those approaches upon soil structure, soil acidity, water tables, disease build up and plant inter-relationships. These became apparent only later. During the 1980s, a move towards more holistic approaches to agricultural production gained momentum as agriculturists, research scientists and academics recognized the inherent problems in the strongly reductionist thinking that permitted the damaging 'productivity' approaches. There is growing interest in 'systems' thinking and organic farming. 'Agriculture' is moving from its 'productivity' stage to a new emphasis on 'sustainability'.

The advances in agricultural practices between each of these stages have called for substantial changes in knowledge and skills, and for changes in the content of agricultural training. They have modified perceptions of what 'agriculture' is. So far, however, much of the new emphasis on 'systems' approaches, now being advocated to move agriculture from 'productivity' to 'sustainability', is still restricted to better integration of different scientific disciplines. 'Agriculture' is about crops, livestock, soils, inputs, markets, etc. 'Agricultural development and sustainability' concern these physical things but, in addition, require not only changes in perceptions, practices and behaviour but also new decisions by farmers everywhere. More knowledge is required to integrate the human and social ingredients of sustainable agriculture into the mix of skills needed to achieve 'sustainability' objectives.

This evolution of agriculture from 'production' and 'productivity' to the sustainable systems approaches now being sought has major implications for agricultural education. However, looking around the world at the specialist resources that both governments and the international donor community have in agricultural education, one finds a remarkable situation. The World Bank, for example, has more than 500 staff positions handling its lending for education and agriculture, but, among these, there is currently only one position for an agricultural education specialist. UNESCO and ILO each has one position in this field; the Inter-American Development Bank, the Africa Development Bank and the Asia Development Bank all have none; IFAD until recently had four but now has none; FAO has nine. While specialist staff positions for agriculturists and educators in these organizations run into thousands, specialist staff for agricultural education number barely a dozen. Agricultural education has been at the periphery of the perceived roles of agriculturists and is only one speciality among many others in Ministries of Education. It has fallen between the two spheres.

This indicates how agriculturists and educators alike have

assumed that their conventional view of 'agriculture' has been correct. The huge investment in agricultural development worldwide – an investment totalling hundreds of billions of dollars – is balanced on an unquestioning trust in the validity of what 'agriculture' and 'agricultural development' have been perceived to be. There is an urgent need for new attention to be paid to agricultural education in order to move agriculture from 'productivity' to 'sustainability'. There is a terrible shortage in governments and in the international development agencies of the necessary skills and policies in this field.

This phenomenon is not confined to agriculture. Dehra Dhun in India, which many have regarded as the premier forestry training institution in Asia, was established in the 1880s. In the last 100 years only two significant reviews of the basic forestry training curriculum took place. A third was made recently to accommodate new 'social forestry' approaches (see page 122).

In the health field, the number of professional health educators among the staff of governments, WHO and other multilateral development agencies is a minute proportion of their medical staff.

Health

The technical orientation of health training was mentioned in Chapter 3. Diagnostic and curative priorities have followed from this, leading to the general association of health services with the treatment and cure of ill-health. Most countries have emphasized urban health care, with well-equipped hospitals and highly trained medical staff and district hospitals, clinics, drug supplies and treatments. These have received a high proportion of public recurrent spending on health. They have been favoured partly as symbols of modernity and partly as a result of bias by aid donors towards capital-intensive projects.

Health infrastructure and curative services are needed. A survey in India, however, showed that 70 per cent of the *causes* of ill-health originated from poor water, sanitation and health practices. Studies in East Africa showed that clean water reduced the incidence of cholera by 90 per cent, of typhoid by 80 per cent, of trachoma by 60 per cent and of leprosy by 50 per cent. The solutions to the causes of ill-health are not the products of investment in hospitals, doctors, clinics and drug supplies. Health workers in most developing countries have contact with those who visit their clinics but generally they are unable to achieve the degree of contact needed with whole communities to achieve the group decision making that is required for widespread changes in health-related behaviour.

If governments' objectives are to improve their countries' health status, how much of their health-related investment should go to the treatment of ill-heath and how much to its prevention? There is a need to redefine 'health' in the context of third world development.

There has been a move towards 'preventative health care' in Ministries of Health worldwide. Few doctors managing these programmes in third world countries have the training and background to deal adequately with the communication processes and behaviour change that ill-health prevention requires. In contrast, a number of UNICEF programmes have been successful in changing health-related behaviour on a large scale – and have shown the essential human/social-oriented nature of the activities required. To do this in some countries, UNICEF has had to set up what has amounted to a parallel service to the traditional Ministry of Health in order to deal with the set of activities needed for the prevention of illness – which are different from those needed for the treatment and cure of ill-health.

There is a need to redefine what 'health' is generally perceived to be, in terms of what health authorities need to know; how they need to be trained; and towards what activities new investment to improve health should be directed. This does not suggest that there is no need for doctors, hospitals, clinics or medical science. It does mean, however, that if the object is to improve a nation's health status and to improve its people's ability to maintain their own health better, significant changes are needed both in orientation of investment in the health sector and in the mix of staff skills in Health Ministries. It also raises questions regarding the roles and the potential of new communication technologies in addressing the large scale changes in perceptions and skills that are now called for.

Nutrition

In 1968, Robert McNamara said:

Two-thirds of the people of the world's diet is so inadequate, in many cases, that they cannot do an effective day's work and, more ominous still, there is growing scientific evidence that the dietary deficiencies of the parent is passed on as mental deficiency to the children. The need has stared us in the face for decades now. But how to help?[2]

His answer at the time was to increase investment in agriculture and in health services – to the tune of many billions of dollars. These solutions were not sufficient. It is estimated that, on average throughout the world, 35,000 people died *each day* in 1990 from chronic malnutrition or starvation.[3] Malnutrition is both a cause and a consequence of underdevelopment. A new perception of the place of nutrition on the agenda for development is needed.

Contributors to malnutrition are numerous. Some are temporary, some are chronic; some, such as drought, famine, wars and increasing land scarcity, are outside local control; some are consequences of development, such as rural to urban migration, urban bias of food pricing and declining export prices. Many others, however, such as food preparation practices, eating habits, neglect of traditional crops and distribution of supplementary food, are within the control of families, communities and/or local authorities and can be influenced by changing knowledge, attitudes and practices within communities.

Numerous causes of malnutrition are related to women and the nature of their poverty. Male migration for employment has increased the already high work load on women in many places. Early pregnancy, many pregnancies and short intervals between births all exacerbate stress on women who may already be malnourished themselves. Low birth weights of babies are the result. Shortening the duration of breast feeding and inadequate supplementary feeding mean that under-nourished children are caught in a degenerating cycle. All of these factors are likewise a product of prevailing beliefs, attitudes and practices which can be changed.

The inability of governments to deal adequately with nutrition is itself an important contributor to the continuing and growing incidence of malnutrition. Food aid has contributed to malnutrition in several countries by affecting market prices of locally grown crops and by reducing the acreage of those crops. The effects of poor nutrition are not easily quantified and valued by economists, so nutrition has tended not to appear in country economic planning. Lack of appreciation, among politicians, policy makers and planners, of the scale of malnutrition and its implications and lack of commitment to nutritional improvement are also major factors in impeding solutions to the global malnutrition crisis.

But there is another, underlying problem. Nutrition's trivial place on the conventional development agenda and the inability of third world governments to deal adequately with it stem from imported attitudes towards nutrition.

Nutrition was much less of a pervasive problem during the development of western countries than it is in the third world today. Malnutrition existed but not on a scale to influence the development of whole economies – as it is now doing in many third world countries. Historically, in temperate western countries, few seriously malnourished people survived the winters, so chronic malnutrition did not exist to the same extent as it does in tropical and subtropical climates now. The reductionism that accompanied the development of the academic disciplines of western education systems reflects the realities of the times. These disciplines were imported by less developed countries. They underlie the present distinctions among agriculturists, medical professionals, educators, local government administrators and others; they influence the organizational structures and development models that flow from them. They do not reflect the different nutritional realities of third world countries.

Responsibility for improving nutrition has fallen somewhere between traditional health, agriculture and education services in most countries. The set of activities which constitute nutritional solutions are scattered among the traditional disciplines and sectors. There is not an adequate constituency for nutrition at any planning level; few countries have an explicit nutrition policy. Donor assistance, dominated by western perceptions of priorities, reinforces orthodox approaches and retards the evolution of staff training, thinking, planning and institutional structures, all of which are needed to respond to countrywide nutritional deficiencies. Too often, malnutrition is thought of as a public health problem and assigned to Ministries of Health. There, typically, it has been a peripheral matter to mainstream health care activities.

Nutrition in third world countries warrants its own slice of the development cake. It needs appropriate institutional structures, budgets and guiding thought. Current praxis lacks a conceptual framework within which to address the dreadful reality that malnutrition is killing more people in third world countries than all of the world's despots put together. The problem – and the solutions – lie in how we *think* about nutrition.

Forestry and Social Forestry

In the 1980s, 'Social Forestry' projects in many countries introduced major programmes of organized tree planting outside designated forest areas. The objectives of these programmes, mentioned in Chapter 4, were principally to meet local needs for fuelwood, building poles and fodder for livestock, at the same time as meeting ecological preservation goals. A feature of these programmes is relevant to our discussion here.

Typically, the Social Forestry programmes comprised three elements:

(a) Supporting Forestry Departments (with more staff, staff training and expansion and financial and logistical inputs) to plant trees on public land beside roads, railways and canals;
(b) Planting by farmers on their own land and on field boundaries;
(c) Planting by communities on wasteland or village woodlots, for conservation purposes and also to provide fuel and fodder for landless households.

A common pattern evolved. Planting by the Forestry Departments on public land went well until it reached the limit of the numbers of staff that the governments could employ and/or supervise. Farmers planted a great many trees. In India in 1986, more than 100 million trees were planted in Gujarat and more than 180 million in Uttar Pradesh (including those planted by the Forestry Department). Evaluation showed, however, that it was predominantly the larger land owners who did so (12 per cent of the farmers in Gujarat and 9 per cent of the farmers in Uttar Pradesh). They had sufficient resources and incentives to respond to the market and to other benefits that they could see from planting trees. The community planting was almost a total failure.

In planting along roads, railways and canals, the Forestry Department staff were basically performing their normal tree-planting and protection functions, just in different locations. Dealing with the communication, education and community decision making needed for the community planting of village woodlots, however, was almost totally outside the training and experience of the forestry staff. Also, the organization of their jobs did not permit the degree of contact with villagers that was necessary to achieve the understanding and the group decision making needed for what was proposed. The nature of 'forestry' had changed but the skills and job definitions of the professional staff had not changed with it.

There were isolated exceptions to the general failure with community planting. In Lucknow district in Uttar Pradesh in India, for example, the local government took over the initiative for supporting community planting from the Forestry Department and achieved impressive results. In Nepal community forestry programmes identified individuals in villages, who already had an interest in trees, to be the local motivators and organizers of the tree planting programmes. Occasionally, the leaders of the local Panchayats took on this role themselves. In each case the results were exceptional.

In a parallel example of a nutrition programme in Aringa in Tanzania, the local government actively supported implementation of the programme, with similar outstanding results.

The critical input in all of these successful cases was that local government involvement internalized the planning and decision making within the local systems and mobilized local resources for what were perceived by the people to be their own programmes.

The subject of community decision making brings us to another field which has been a 'non-discipline' in the mainstream of development investment.

Community mobilization

The emphasis of 'development' on physical, technical and economic fields has achieved partial success in development to date. While investment has focused on the priorities deriving from macro-economic considerations, a much less conspicuous, parallel activity has been moving forward all over the world – mostly in small and isolated programmes at community level. Generally, these programmes have been run by NGOs. They have helped communities to establish a degree of holistic, self-sustaining development which the fragmented efforts of the technical ministries alone have not achieved. Analysis of these programmes and of the staff that they have used shows that they have been successful in dealing with the human/social elements of development that are outside the skills and experience of technically trained professionals.

In 1984, over 200 NGOs from all over the world, led by the Institute of Cultural Affairs (operating worldwide but based in Brussels), brought together in New Delhi in India practitioners from 350 programmes in 55 countries. The programmes had been selected by their governments (from more than 1200 candidates) as examples of success in achieving self-sustaining development at village level. The object was to gather together a sufficient body of experience and expertise to demonstrate to governments, donor agencies and all involved in development work the activities needed to achieve community mobilization.

By analysing the 350 programmes represented in New Delhi, participants showed that, in varying degrees and mostly unintentionally, all of the programmes had included a common set of activities. The programmes had assisted the local people in: gathering and assessing their own data; defining their priority objectives; identifying common interest groups; planning activities to address their own priorities; mobilizing their own resources; and improving skills, management and internal and external communication. This set of activities was shown to be replicable and to form an additional ingredient to the necessary physical, financial and technical inputs on which most development effort has focused.

We have had clearly established sets of activities that constitute 'road building', 'primary education', 'agricultural research' and the like, but have lacked an equivalent set of activities for 'community mobilization'.

One outcome was a programme in the Philippines, specifically designed to demonstrate that the World Bank could fund this replicable set of activities. It had remarkable results at village level, showing how quickly villagers would mobilize their own resources when development objectives reflected their own priorities and how inexpensive the catalytic input to help them to do so could be.

We can link the conclusions in New Delhi with new perceptions of information and communication and with digital technology systems. The common set of essential activities above is the same as most of the human and institutional functions listed in Table 1.1 on page 8. The data storage, processing, multi-media communication and interactivity of the technology can assist every one of this set of activities. This further indicates the potential of the technology for helping to empower village people and local governments for their own development.

Community mobilization and administration is the 'bottom end' of local government. The technologies and a basis of thinking are now available for addressing village mobilization on a large scale. This can change traditional perceptions of and approaches for, local government and decentralized, community-based development.

Women's development

New priority in government and development agencies is being given to women's development. It is extraordinary that after forty years of development investment in the name of benefiting the people in recipient countries, we now need special programmes to address the needs of half of them. This is simply yet another illustration of the extent to which the needs of people have been overlooked in conventional thinking and approaches for development.

In addressing this objective through existing systems, each new project in agriculture, health, urban development, education, etc. receives an add-on called 'women's development'. These add-ons are needed where insufficient account has been taken of the special needs of women in relation to the physical objectives of each sector. Just as the sum of the traditional technical sectors does not add up to all that is needed for sustainable development, so too the sum of the separate add-ons in each does not add up to the totality of women's development.

This was demonstrated in the World Bank's first, free-standing project to address 'the development of the productivity and welfare of women', which was designed with assistance from the International Labour Organization. This showed that it is possible to address 'women's development' as an objective of development in its own right – instead of just as a peripheral activity in the achievement of agricultural or other production oriented goals.

(The country concerned was Somalia where the need to improve the conditions for women is extreme. Unfortunately, civil strife has prevented implementation of the project.)

The approach and components of the project are very similar to those of the successful community mobilization programmes. They involved working with women to identify their priority needs – as they perceived them – and incorporating the opportunity to express these needs and the means for responding to them, into the local planning processes. The common nature of processes involved indicates that if the identity of community mobilization were recognized as a legitimate ingredient of development and given its proper place on the development agenda, it would automatically include the needs of women. We would not have to make women's needs a special objective of development, although we would still require people skilled in identifying and addressing women's priorities within holistic approaches to community mobilization.

Water

Water has been plentiful in temperate zones. It has been possible to take its availability for granted. Like nutrition, water has a different reality in the tropics and sub-tropics from the temperate zones where conventional scientific thinking about water evolved. A World Health Organization study showed that 79 per cent of rural people in Africa do not have access to safe water but that 80 per cent of the money spent on water supply went to urban areas, as did 97 per cent of the investment on sewerage. We need to re-think 'water' in development. An example will illustrate the point.

Twelve years ago, piped water was available for only four hours a day in some parts of the capital of one north African country. The city's expansion and its industrial development had exceeded the capacity of the large catchment area from which it drew its water. The next large catchment was many miles away. This was dammed and water from that dam was pumped into the catchment of the first dam and from there supplied to the city. Water was plentiful again.

The second dam is rapidly silting up from the soil erosion in that catchment; the alluvium being pumped into the first dam is silting up that one too. The silt load has worn down the pumps in the second dam, so that they now need replacing, and is damaging the pumps in the first dam and the distribution infrastructure as well. After twelve years and an investment of $US2 billion, parts of the capital city now have only two hours of water a day. The cost of bringing water from a more distant catchment is prohibitive.

The solution for a sustainable supply of water no longer lies in dams, pumps and pipes nor in the work of water engineers. It lies in changing the behaviour of the 200,000 households in both catchment areas. This requires education, assistance and incentives to help them to do so. The set of activities which previously we equated with water supply (dams, pumps, pipes, etc.) is no longer sufficient.

Educating people *about* natural resource preservation, however, is not enough. The education and training to *achieve* that preservation is needed. Interactive technology has immense potential as a tool for assisting communities to enter their own data on their own resources and to process it and weigh up alternative solutions. It carries the learning process into practical application in specific situations and can then provide technical instructional materials to suit the conditions of those situations. This capacity to help individuals, groups and communities to manage their own resource is being shown to have a remarkable 'mobilizing' effect.

The above example is not an isolated case. It is estimated that forty countries worldwide will exceed the capacities of their water supplies within the next fifteen years if current water usage and destruction of the catchment areas continues.

Water has been abundant for most people in more developed economies until now. It has been a 'neutral' factor in most of the disciplines for which water is a factor. New attention to 'water', to its roles and growing confines in many fields of activity, is now needed in all of those disciplines. Already, in a few countries, planning decisions are not being based first on competing needs for capital but on competing needs for water by industry, agriculture and social users.

Water shortage is not just a third world problem. Big cities in the most advanced countries, where clean water has been taken for granted by their populations until now, are facing growing problems with their water supplies. Massive re-education programmes on water use and preservation are called for, together with tools to help families and communities to understand and manage their use of water and to allocate limited water optimally. Digital systems will have an important role in doing this.

Environment

'Environment' means different things to different people. It can mean water pollution, litter, clean air, wildlife preservation, ozone depletion, deforestation, soil conservation, tourist damage, population increase, destruction of mountain ecology, global warming, declining water tables, and countless other things depending on where one is and to whom one is speaking. It is a catch-all phrase, like 'Basic Needs' and 'Institutional Development', under whose banner a variety of new activities can be justified to fill gaps in orthodox development approaches.

All of these fields of activity require urgent action. Look again at the list. All are physical! In the Brundtland Commission report,[4] we find the same phenomenon. Each chapter discusses a different physical topic, such as industrial pollution, deforestation or global warming. The language emphasizes the physical problems rather than the human and institutional actions needed for their solution.

A UNDP poster captures the opposite perception. The picture is of hot, desolate sand dunes. The caption beneath says quite simply: 'Weather does not make deserts – people do!' This perception is missing from much of the effort now being directed towards environmental preservation. The following example illustrates the problem in a different way.

A major donor agency recently established an Environmental Department in response both to criticism of neglect of the environmental consequences of its development investments and to governments' needs for assistance in this field. The Department is now helping countries with environmental policies. In one of the first African countries to receive this assistance, foreign consultants were commissioned to help. Conscious of the need for a comprehensive analysis, they travelled widely throughout the country and held detailed discussions with many people.

They wrote up their conclusions and recommendations which were presented at a seminar in the capital city some months later. A broad range of government agencies were represented. After opening the seminar, the senior government official chairing the proceedings surprised the visitors by saying,

'We are disappointed by this proposal, it does not reflect the context of our country.'

The consultants defended the proposal, showing how it took account of land areas, soils, rainfall, numbers of people, numbers of cattle, crop production, forests and much else. They pointed to its recommendations for more investment in grazing control, cattle improvement, land planning, soil conservation, water protection and conservation education in schools. The government officials replied by saying, 'But we are doing these things already.' And so they were – mostly on a small scale in scattered projects in different parts of the country. The government officials saw no new solutions in the proposals.

What was missing and what the government's technical staff were not able to articulate adequately (for the reasons outlined in Chapter 3), was attention to the whole human/social dimension of environmental preservation needs in their country. A small section on 'environmental education in schools' was the only activity in the whole proposal that focused directly on action needed to change knowledge and behaviour.

If we look again at the interpretations of 'environment' given above, one thing is common to all of them: the human under-standings and capabilities, which are needed at individual, household and community levels and at all levels of government in all fields, and the means by which to develop such understanding and capability. If 'environment' is approached and described from the viewpoint of human behaviour, not physical phenomena, a very different emphasis for new investment emerges. It creates a framework of thinking in which the actions needed for environmental preservation and local management can not only be defined but also achieved.

CONCLUSION

The realities of third world countries differ from those in western, temperate countries in which current disciplines, organizational structures and the rationale underlying development approaches evolved. This calls for questioning and review of the accepted disciplines and sectors in place for development and of approaches that follow from current orthodoxy. We must allow such questioning, in order to appreciate that the 'shape' of the traditional disciplines and sectors in the context of the realities of third world countries is different from that of the ruling conventional wisdom to date. We can then create the necessary environment of thinking and policies in which to overcome the confines inherent in the systems now in place for development. We can cut the 'development cake' differently. We can make a new paradigm for development attainable, in which both physical/economic and human/institutional objectives are achievable. The nature of that paradigm and how to get there are the subjects of the final chapter.

Chapter 6

A new paradigm: a realm of new opportunity

The way to look at the future is to begin to look at the empowering of individuals, not just the empowering of institutions. We are starting to see the real need for a paradigm shift, the shift in the model of the way in which we look at things.[1]

Key points in the preceding chapters include the following.

1   Increasing GNP has been the guiding star for 'mainstream' investment in development. Pursuit of this objective has put in place systems to achieve physical elements of economic production but has neglected the systems and activities needed to develop people and institutions. The primary object of development is the development of people, in order, among other things, to increase GNP.

2   All communication systems can carry information on any topic (other than systems depending on narrowly trained human beings). Conventional approaches to development have tried to make each technical sector its own communication channel and so have fragmented approaches for the development and use of communication systems.

3   The combination of the different communication systems constitutes a communication 'sector' in its own right. Conventional thinking about the nature of 'development' has not included this understanding.

4   The reductionism of western education systems, the disciplines and institutional structures that have followed from them and the way in which these have programmed us to think underlie the persistent difficulties that mainstream investment has had in addressing the human/social dimension of

    development and in recognizing the communication sector in development.

5   Digital technology systems introduce a new communication medium which is capable of assisting with the broad range of activities that together constitute the human/institutional dimension of development. Through investment in a single informatics system, it will be possible to support a wide variety of human development functions. This provides a basis for a new, cross-sectoral approach to the human/social dimension of development. It will change conventional perceptions of what 'development' is.

6   An unquestioning belief in the validity of the traditional disciplines in the form in which they have developed in temperate climates has given low priority to, or actually excluded, the different realities of third world societies where tropical and sub-tropical climates prevail and the state of development of human capital is vastly different.

7   We can move beyond the confines of current orthodoxy and of present disciplines, structures and approaches to create an environment of thought in which it will be possible to address the human and institutional prerequisites of sustainable development which have proved so elusive until now.

The implications of the combination of the above are bigger than their sum. For example, large scale programmes to introduce generic informatics systems will create corresponding employment; recognition of the communication sector will open up new investment opportunities; the skills of the social disciplines will be needed to asssist in developing the community uses of the technology. But there is more than this.

    The development of railways did far more than create employment for railway builders, steel industries and equipment suppliers. Railways profoundly affected trade, travel, human migration, military strategies and much else. Digital systems for public use have similarly far reaching implications. Their newness will affect economic activity through employment generation in their own establishment and through the new market opportunities that they will create for entertainment, banking and other services, advertising, distance learning and so on. They will also affect economic activity (a) by means of their capacity to create and improve marketable skills, (b) by increasing efficiency through their management applications, and (c) by bringing into the marketplace many of the hundreds of millions of people who have been at the fringes of economic activity to date.

The new systems introduce a new item in the infrastructure for development. Traditional approaches and economic theory will need to adjust to the new realities which they and new perceptions of the communication sector will create.

DUAL REALITY

The new systems will come about rapidly, driven by their potential profitability, by the new markets that they create for the information and entertainment industries and by the new solutions that they offer in the social sector. Governments, donor agencies and the whole development fraternity are therefore at the point of a dual reality: the reality of what is possible now, within the existing systems and conventional wisdom, and the new reality, with its different possibilities, which will soon be introduced. Five-year projects being planned now will be completed in six or seven years' time. Informatics systems for public use will be in place in many countries (on a limited scale) before then and their planning will be far advanced in many others.

Planning in all of the conventional sectors now needs to accommodate this dual reality. New investment not only needs to continue to support what is currently possible within existing systems and conventional wisdom but also needs to create the conditions to accelerate the introduction of the new reality. This calls for planning to be undertaken with a vision of the future. Most development investment has been planned and justified on the basis of measurable evidence from the past.

Changes of the sorts implied above pose challenges to current policies and conventional wisdom for development. We all tend to oppose challenges to the status quo; strong forces maintain it. An understanding of those forces helps in defining (a) the sorts of activities that will accelerate the changes that are now possible, and (b) activities that are likely to retard those objectives.

This final chapter discusses these subjects and also looks at the urgency of the need to achieve change; it considers briefly the sorts of opportunities that open up with the introduction of a new basis of thinking about the development of people and of the role of the communication sector in so doing.

Opposing change

We 'hear' and accept information which supports our current thinking and tend to reject information which questions it. This is part of our natural defence and survival mechanisms. Moreover, psychologists tell us that the higher our self esteem, the harder it is for us to accept that we may be wrong. The same applies to institutions. Consequently, managers of prominent organizations usually defend current approaches and their underlying rationale. These have been the basis on which they have staked their professional reputations. Ironically, the very people most committed to maintaining the status quo are those from whom we need and expect new leadership to change it.

If professional people and prominent organizations have such difficulty in accepting change and if change is now possible and is urgently needed across a broad spectrum of development activity, how can we proceed?

Thomas Khun can help with the insights that he provides to the nature of paradigms of thinking and to the effects of significant change in the environment for our thinking and action.[2]

PARADIGMS AND PARADIGM SHIFTS

Thomas Khun, in his *Theory of Scientific Revolution*, described the characteristics of paradigms of thinking and technology and of advances (shifts) from one paradigm to the next. An understanding of the essential nature of paradigms can help in anticipating and accepting the changes that informatics and new perceptions of the communication sector will bring about.

'Paradigm' is used here to mean the environment in which we think, reason and act at any particular time. The 'boundaries' of paradigms are set by the stage of scientific discovery and of general knowledge, by the applications of new technologies and by the prevailing conventional wisdom and accepted social practice pertaining at any particular time. The boundaries change with every new scientific discovery. A few of these changes have been very significant, leading to major shifts in paradigm: the printing press, the harnessing of steam power, electricity, the internal combustion engine, the telephone, aeroplanes and antibiotics, for example.

Even small changes in technology lead to modest changes in

paradigm. Consider the introduction of aluminium cans to take the place of bottles for beer and soft drinks. This has affected the behaviour of a great many people in small ways. It represents a shift in the environment of what has been possible for beverage manufacturers, consumers, transporters, retailers, recyclers and advertisers alike. One can see flattened cans used as roofing tiles in West Africa and the Carribean; as street paving to reduce the dust in remote desert towns in Arabia; and as lining for irrigation channels in the mountains of Nepal. Aluminium cans have brought about a change in paradigm in the modest fields of activity that they affect.

When looking at the social applications of digital technology and at a new framework of thinking for the human dimension of development, we are considering a change in paradigm of enormous proportions. A knowledge of the critical features of paradigm changes will therefore help in anticipating and recognizing the processes involved.

Thomas Khun says that new paradigms:

(a) Build on, rather than replace, preceding ones;
(b) Are empowering;
(c) Introduce new language;
(d) Are pervasive;
(e) Cannot be fully described until they have been achieved.

Let us consider the practical applications of these five features as they relate to a new understanding of the nature of the communication sector and of the place and potential of digital technologies in that sector.

First, new paradigms *build on what exists* (see Figure 6.1). The new reasoning, action and investment that emanates from recognition of the communication sector and from social applications of informatics systems will move 'development' (as shown in Figure 6.1) from A to B, not from A to C.

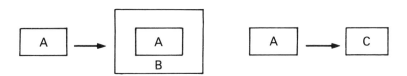

Figure 6.1 A new paradigm builds on what exists.

Thomas Khun's classic illustration of this was the advent of the steam engine. Until 1776, everything that humanity had done was confined to what was possible using the power of wind, water, gravity, animals (including humans) or the sun. Sophisticated uses of cogs, pulleys, chains, belts and levers had evolved to transfer power. The steam engine gave humanity a new form of power. But it did not replace existing forms of power, nor did it render cogs, pulleys, chains or levers obsolete. Instead, it provided a new physical and conceptual environment in which to plan and use them.

A conceptual framework within which the role of communication is recognized and valued will create the environment of thought and policies for new investment in the communication sector and in new informatics systems in particular. Large scale replication of isolated, successful initiatives in the use of digital technologies will be possible.

Second, a paradigm shift is *empowering*. It creates conceptual and physical environments in which new things are possible and releases people from the confines of earlier paradigms. We can see this by looking back at previous major paradigm shifts. The printing press released people from the confines of handwritten script; the steam engine released people from the confines of wind, water and animal power; electricity and internal combustion engines introduced whole realms of new innovation. Each opened up new horizons. New concepts which address the communication process in development and which draw resources from the whole information industry into the mainstream of development are particularly empowering because (a) they affect many forms of communication, (b) they can affect everyone, and (c) they constitute an essential, missing ingredient in the development recipe. Being involved in a major paradigm shift is a very exciting time to be around!

Third, a new paradigm creates its own *language*. This involves both new words to describe the new technology and a broadening of the meaning of existing words. Consider again the analogy with steam engines and railways. One needed new verbal distinctions for locomotives and their cylinders, pistons, valves and boilers and for railways with their rails, sleepers, signals, cuttings, embankments, carriages, wagons and couplings before one could know about and discuss these new phenomena. (Note the new meanings given to old words.) As discussed in Chapter 5, changes are now taking place in the nature of what will still be called 'education', 'health', 'agriculture', 'nutrition' and even 'development' itself. The fact that we are already finding the need to adopt different or broader meanings for these words confirms that we are now at the point of a major paradigm shift. One could not operate in the paradigm that the steam engine introduced without the necessary language. Similarly, with the advent of digital systems, our vocabularies now need to include such terms as bytes, monitors, CD-ROMs, management software, data compression, viruses and informatics. Until people in responsible positions acquire this language, they will not be equipped to operate in the new paradigm. Investment in an educational process is called for to overcome this basic obstacle and to accelerate the shift in paradigms which is now possible.

Fourth, new paradigms of thinking and action are *pervasive*. Looking back over the major technological advances mentioned above, one can see how, directly or indirectly, they affected whole societies. (Consider the pervasiveness of the aluminium can and the small changes of behaviour that it has brought about!) Technologies and concepts that deal with information and communication have applications in every field of human endeavour.

At first, the scale of the paradigm shift which is now before us can seem daunting and threatening. By its nature, however, it will open up new opportunities in every field for everyone who is prepared to exploit them. An important feature of a focus on communication and the development of people is that it will, for the first time, create a place in the mainstream of development for sociologists, community development specialists, anthropologists, communication and management professionals, community development workers and the whole information industry.

Early recognition of this pervasiveness is particularly relevant in the case of the new electronic delivery systems. From an operational perspective, if those systems are to be financially viable, their uses have to be developed over a wide range of applications concurrently. They must be thought about holistically, and be used multi-functionally. This will require cross-sectoral cooperation in their establishment. It will also entail inputs from governments, academia, the hardware, software and telecommunication industries and the financial and business communities. It will create new opportunities for all of them.

It is significant that, in the United States, it has taken an initiative by the US Chambers of Commerce, with access across disciplines and sectors and with support from various government agencies, a White House Committee and the military, to achieve the cross-sectoral planning for the major programme to introduce a national software delivery system.

Finally, 'We cannot accurately predict the content of a new paradigm until we get there.' Aristotle described submarines and flying machines. Until they actually existed, however, no one could say for certain what they looked like or what they could actually do. It is important that planners and policy makers understand this feature of new paradigms. All of the different pieces of the puzzle referred to throughout this book and documented in the literature cited point to the nature of different parts of the new paradigm but we cannot quantify the parts until they are put together. The statistics and cost data that planners and economists demand cannot and will not exist for a new paradigm until it has come about. By requiring proven figures to quantify change before it has happened and before giving their support to new programmes, such people retard change.

During a lecture on Science and Technology in 1989, Lord Perry of Walton, founder of the Open University, described the university's inception:

> There was only one way that the Open University could be started. It started big and with no pilot experiments. It was a gigantic act of faith. A new, communication-based education system can only be started if there is a further act of faith several orders of magnitude larger.

An act of faith by strong leaders is needed, which is based on the sum of the pieces of the available thinking and experience in the social applications of digital technology and on experience with more familiar communication systems. Without such leadership, existing institutions are bound to continue only to do more in development at the fringes of what they have done already, which cannot carry development much beyond the point to which those approaches have brought us.

On a lighter note, we can describe paradigms in a different way.[3] If we consider the universe of what is 'knowable', we can distinguish three categories:

(a) What we currently know – and know we know;
(b) What we know that we do not know, and
(c) What we do not know that we don't know.

These are illustrated in Figure 6.2, in which the circle represents the universe of what is knowable. (The proportions cannot be accurate because we do not know how much we don't know!)

Research and experiment push the frontiers of knowledge into areas that we know we do not know and convert what we know that we do not know into what we know. These advances permit successive marginal improvements in current thinking and approaches in every field.

Occasionally, often by accident, discoveries and perceptive individuals lead us into new fields. They expose small fractions of something new; something that we did not know that we did not know. Some of these, of which digital technologies are an example, have ramifications in almost every field of human activity. It is in these advances and discoveries that new paradigms are born.

We now know what informatics systems are. We know that they have very wide applications but do not yet know exactly what those will be. The exposure of a small piece of what we did not know that

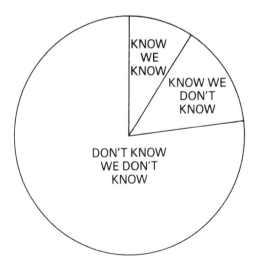

Figure 6.2 Our knowledge of the universe of knowledge.

we did not know has uncovered a much larger realm of what we now know that we do not know. We do not yet know the details of the practicalities of all of the applications of these technologies but, now that we know that we do not know, we can justify investment to find out. A first step is an educational one to educate policy makers and planners (who do not yet know what they do not know), so that they are more familiar with this new realm. They will then know better what they need to know and will allocate funds for the work required to define, explore and demonstrate the nature of this new field.

At the point at which we now stand in entering the new paradigm, investment to create new knowledge and understanding of its concepts and technologies is more important than the technologies themselves.

CONFINES OF THE PRESENT PARADIGM

A great deal has been achieved in development within the present paradigm for development. Improvements in health, transportation, water supply and literacy, increased production and the green revolution are just a few. Do we need to change the paradigm?

Change has occurred in order to achieve all of these successes. The changes have involved advances within each technical discipline and sector. But these advances within each technical sector have not changed the ruling physical/technical/economic parameters of the overall paradigm formed by traditional, rationalistic, western thinking. As shown in Chapter 3, those parameters have excluded (unintentionally) the language, skills and approaches (the environment of thinking and reasoning) by which to address adequately the human dimension of self-sustaining development.

Separately, each technical sector has attempted to tackle the human/social elements for success in its own programmes. Evaluations in each sector refer to difficulties of 'beneficiary participation', 'management', 'communication', 'skill deficiencies', 'institutional constraints' and 'administrative weaknesses'. Typically these are referred to as 'problems', while physical and economic goals are referred to as 'objectives'. A different perception of the human dimension of development enables us to define the former as objectives too and to address them accordingly. To someone equipped with a toothpick and a hairbrush, removing a spark plug in an engine would be a 'problem'. Equipped with the right tools, removing the spark plug becomes an objective, not a problem. The paradigm in which we have all grown up has not given technical, economic and financial professionals the right tools (either conceptually or physically) to deal adequately with the human dimension of development. Each sector, individually, has been unable to break out of the confines of the overall, dominating paradigm.

Two examples illustrate the need for an understanding of the confines of paradigms.

Japan and Australia have embarked on a huge cooperative programme to build a city of the future. Various states in Australia competed in drawing up proposals. One state attempted a highly innovative approach. Instead of beginning with the conventional planning of buildings, roads, water supplies, etc., those responsible recognized the central role that information and communication technology will have in the future. They attempted to plan their city on the basis of the functions of a digital information transfer system and all of its applications. Distinguished consultants were commissioned to advise (separately) on future applications of new technology in education, health, business, finance, recreation and other fields. A pile of expensive reports was produced containing much excellent material. But, despite the input of all this expertise, those responsible for the project felt that it did not provide them with a basis for a different approach to their planning. Something was missing.

The problem was that, by seeking advice separately in each orthodox field, the planners had restricted themselves and their consultants to the prevailing paradigm. Each report examined details only within the boundaries of its own discipline. None of them could stand back from their respective sectors and show how the public use of a generic informatics system, with its cross-sectoral application to communication, learning, management and entertainment, will change the 'shape' and nature of those sectors, creating solutions to problems that fall between and across them.

When this was pointed out to the planners and their attention was focused on how generic systems will permit new approaches that break out of the confines of the traditional perceptions of 'education', 'health', local government and recreation and so change their nature, they were suddenly enabled to move into a new realm. Much of the valuable material in the reports could be interpreted and applied in a new light, making new solutions possible. The data were usable in a different paradigm.

In 1989, the World Bank embarked on the ambitious task of drawing up a 'Long Term Perspective Plan for Africa' to the year 2020. A team of economists was given the job. They gathered large quantities of data and made projections of population increase, food requirements, market trends, capital needs, soil erosion, industrial development, GNP and much else. They produced a draft document but this was judged to be inadequate. It did not provide sufficient solutions for poverty alleviation, self-sustaining development and other chronic difficulties. It was thought that Africans could help and so distinguished people from Africa were invited to assist the effort. They did so and a second draft was prepared. This was still found to be inadequate. A second team of authors (also economists) replaced the first. They re-distilled the material and added their own perceptions. Their draft contained a small section headed 'Human Resource Development' but this equated human resource development with basic health and basic education, plus a small piece on 'women's development'.

After further toil, they produced a new draft which devoted a whole section to 'Investing in People: Toward Human-Centered Development'. It states: 'For the longer term, and by 2020, African countries could realistically aim for universal food security, primary education, and primary health care.' The study's thirty year projection into the future contained no reference whatever to the revolution taking place in the social applications of digital technologies, to their potential for assisting the full range of essential human and institutional development functions or to new perceptions of the communication process in development.

The problem again was one of paradigms. The content of successive versions of the report were extrapolations from the past and present, confined by old language about traditional school and health systems and by other limits of the prevailing environment of thinking and action. The document contained no recognition of the inherent confines of those systems, and so struggled to find solutions which do not exist within them. The African advisers helped to broaden the perspectives of the study but were unable to move it outside the confines of the dominating paradigm.

Use of these two examples is not a criticism of what took place. The outcomes were predictable and inevitable while the reasoning was locked within the structures, language and confines of the old paradigm. One can find elements of the same phenomenon in a wide range of development policy documents. They all illustrate the need to achieve an understanding of (a) the underlying conceptual obstacles that are obstructing progress in development and preventing the achievement of the human and social prerequisites of sustainablility, and (b) the new opportunities that open up when we break out of those confines.

THE URGENCY

There is great urgency about achieving the new paradigm into which the world can now move. This advance is needed for all of the familiar reasons, such as poverty and debt alleviation, equity, employment, north–south trade and sustainability, but there is another cause for urgency.

We are all aware of environmental degradation, population increase, the spread of AIDS, increasing unemployment and crime, and other nightmares of the 1990s but we are not fully aware of how serious these things are. This is not because we are ill-informed or are disinterested; it is because of how we think.

Virtually all of our experience and comprehension of size and growth is linear. We think of and measure length, weight, height, time (for example) in one dimension only. This is the basis of our mental 'programming'. Much growth in nature, however, is not linear but exponential. We may know this but (with the possible exception of a few individuals) it is not part of our normal comprehension.

The following example illustrates the point. Imagine fifty people sitting in a small hall or meeting room. They are in five rows, ten seats in each row. One sheet of ordinary typing paper is given to the first person in the front row. He or she is asked to add a similar sheet of paper and to pass on the two sheets to the person beside him/her. The second person receives two sheets, adds two and hands on four. The third person receives four, adds four and hands on eight; the next passes on 16, the next 32, and so on up and down the five rows all the way to the fiftieth person. He or she stacks all of the sheets on top of one another. How high will the pile be? The pile will reach not just to the ceiling or the

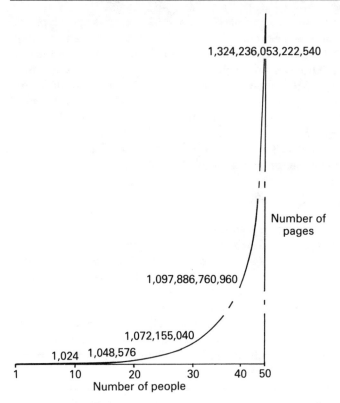

Figure 6.3 Growth of the pile of paper.
If the graph were drawn accurately to the scale shown for the
number of pages after 30 people had added their contributions,
the point for 40 people would be some 40 feet off the page and the
point for 50 people would be approximately 48 miles away!

roof or the mountain tops or even the moon but almost to the
nearest planet.

We have no difficulty envisioning the five rows with ten seats in
each row or the fifty people successively passing paper down the
rows. This is linear. We do have great difficulty in visualizing
accurately the growth of the pile of paper. The pile will grow
exponentially but our brains have not been taught to think in this
way. We can graph the data as shown above, which helps us to
comprehend the increasing rate of growth of the pile of paper in
the hall, but the rate and scale of growth is probably not what we
had visualized.

The point of this example is that the nightmares referred to above, which are responding to natural phenomena, are growing (or deteriorating) exponentially. Their pace is accelerating in a way that we have difficulty in comprehending and anticipating. Consider the spread of AIDS: from being almost unknown only a decade ago, the disease is now infecting over 20 per cent of the adult population in a number of countries and even more in Uganda, Rwanda and parts of neighbouring countries. Its expansion has been slowed as it has approached the norms of promiscuity in those societies. Until that point its expansion has been exponential.

Environmental degradation is accelerating in this way and is therefore worse than we actually imagine. The US military has been photographing parts of the world in great detail from satellites for more than fifteen years. The Environmental Protection Agency in Washington DC obtained this material for selected areas of the world and put the pictures into a time series to show the change in vegetation over the fifteen years. The disappearance of the vegetation during this period is appalling but seeing the way in which the rate of degradation accelerates towards the end of the period is terrifying. And, of course, it is continuing to accelerate.

Humanity has caused these problems and only changes in human behaviour can control them. We now have the technology and a conceptual framework for a major advance in achieving the communication needed by humanity to do so. It is with the developmental communication processes and the potential of the integrated use of all communication systems that governments – all governments – now need to be most concerned. The urgency of directing resources to break out of the confines of the prevailing physical and economic paradigm and to put in place the skills, systems and approaches to help people and communities to improve their management of their own destinies can barely be overstated.

NEW OPPORTUNITIES

We saw earlier that new paradigms are pervasive and that a paradigm which expands the present boundaries of information and communication will reach into every field of human activity. By that same token, it will create new opportunities in every field too. There is not room to address all of these opportunities here but we can outline major categories in which particularly important and far reaching possibilities exist.

Academia

It will fall to educationists to provide intellectual leadership in understanding and defining the changes that new perceptions will bring about; to review existing curricula in all disciplines in which changing people's behaviour is significant; to develop in-service training programmes for staff in all government social services; to address education for adults; to integrate the use of interactive technology into instructional approaches and to realize this potential in distance learning.

The information industry

The way is open to expand telecommunication capacity and coverage; to develop low cost hardware and its assembly on a large scale; to develop touch screen and multi-media technology to benefit the millions of people who cannot read; to develop countries' capacity to produce or adapt instructional and management software to suit their own conditions and cultures and to work with governments and donor agencies to establish mechanisms for integrating the information industry into the mainstream of development.

Trusts and foundations

The structures and budgets of existing governments and donor agencies are committed to their present objectives and practices. Few unallocated funds exist for major new initiatives outside those orthodox activities. Foundations and trusts have a critical, catalytic role in helping to introduce the new concepts for the communication sector and to support demonstrations and pilot programmes in the many fields of application that the new approaches will open up.

Business and finance

The integration of the skills and resources of the information industry, new investment in existing communication systems and the development of digital 'utilities' will create new opportunities for the business and financial sectors in every country. Needs for electricity in villages throughout the third world offer enormous opportunities for the solar industry. Chambers of Commerce and Industry Associations will have important roles in creating understanding among their members of these new needs and opportunities.

The media

The media have a major role to play in raising awareness of new perceptions of the central role of the development of people, of informatics systems, of the communication sector, of new experience in these fields and of all that this will bring about. The media need to be used deliberately to do this. By doing so, the potential of media can be used in a directly developmental role.

Governments

The new paradigm opens up opportunities for new approaches and solutions in many of the fields in which governments almost everywhere are facing most difficulty. Governments have opportunities for new political leadership, policies and strategies. They can address the communication sector and can assess and strengthen all communication channels. They can increase the efficiency of their existing systems and address new priorities which lie outside the expertise and mandates of those systems. Major programmes are called for to retrain and reorient staff of technical services and to review jobs in these services in light of new roles for technical staff in relation to major changes in the whole communication process in development. Governments need to provide leadership and to create the environments and incentives for these things to happen.

Donor agencies

The challenge for donor agencies will be to support all of the above and to equip themselves to do so. Morale in the major agencies has fallen seriously in the last decade as evidence has grown of the inadequacies of further investment in conventional approaches. More and more resources have been allocated to studies to explain shortcomings or to justify approaches of the past. The new paradigm will open up new avenues through which to achieve previous objectives and to make new objectives possible.

The world lacks a body to do for the development of the social applications of digital systems and of the communication sector generally what FAO does for agriculture, WHO does for health, UNESCO does for education or CGIAR[4] does for agricultural research. A new institution is called for to provide a global resource in this new field. It would not need expensive structures and a large full time staff. It would use communication technology to link workers internationally in each of the new fields of application in the social sector; would gather data on successful experience; would work with existing technical agencies, NGOs and the information industry and would assist governments with new policies, research and the design of new programmes. Donor agencies, major foundations and the information industry need to combine to establish such a body which can serve all of them (as was done to establish the CGIAR to serve the agricultural sector). This calls for leadership from the world's major development agencies.

These opportunities for everyone may read like a panacea. The technology *per se*, is not a panacea (as stated in Chapter 3) but, in a limited way, a new paradigm for thought and action is. It opens up a whole range of activities and new solutions from which conventional thinking, old traditions and the limits of previous technology and thinking have excluded us until now. A new paradigm is not a total panacea; it has its own confines. These, and what lies beyond them, we can only explore as the new paradigm is achieved.

It is reasonable for the reader to ask three questions. Is the new paradigm inevitable? Will the forces driving change carry us into the new era automatically? Can we get on with our own affairs and let others change paradigms?

The demand for the new paradigm will far exceed the demand for earlier paradigm shifts. It concerns a change that can benefit the whole world, by changing the focus of development from the development of things to the development of people. It offers new opportunities and solutions in fields affecting humanity's survival. At the same time, the new paradigm will be driven by a profit motive in the same way that profit drove the industrial revolution. The technology that it requires is already available; much infrastructure which it needs is already in place and funding will be forthcoming from both public and private sector sources. The new paradigm will come about very much faster than earlier paradigm shifts of equivalent magnitude.

In this light, the answer to the first question above is 'Yes'. The answer to the second is a qualified 'Yes'. The pace of change will be influenced by (a) how quickly the environment of understanding needed to advance beyond our present paradigm can be achieved, and (b) how soon and how seriously this is addressed.

The answer to the third question depends on who the reader is. Only for a total nobody can the answer to this question be 'Yes'. The need for us to help to accelerate the introduction of the new paradigm and the solutions for humanity that it contains is directly proportional to our influence, contacts and position. Since a total nobody will not have read this book to this point, the answer to the third question must be 'No'.

Following a recent presentation on the subject of this book at an International Symposium, a participant commented: 'I had resigned myself to thinking that the future for humanity was hopeless. I now believe that we have a basis for hope.' The challenge facing the world now and the responsibility facing development practitioners, and those in academia, in the information industry, in the media and in decision making positions everywhere is to strive to realize the hope that the new paradigm offers.

Winston Churchill wrote:

Occasionally in the course of their lives, men stumble over a piece of the truth. Most pick themselves up and hurry on as though nothing had happened.

Winston Churchill would surely have considered a new perception of the communication sector in development and the hope that it offers for addressing the development of people to be a piece of the truth. He would have urged us to examine, understand and act upon it.

Notes

1 The revolution

1 *New Information Technologies and Development* (New York: UN Center for Science and Technology Department, 1986).
2 Robert S. McNamara, President of the World Bank, 1968–81; *Addresses of Robert S. McNamara 1968–1981* (Baltimore and London: Johns Hopkins University Press, 1981).
3 'Hidden hand' was a term used by Adam Smith in his *The Wealth of Nations,* written in 1776.
4 Professor S. C. Dube's book, *Modernization and Development: the Search for Alternative Paradigms,* includes an extensive bibliography of significant work on which his conclusions are based.
5 Ibid.
6 Jamshid Gharajedaghi and Russel Ackoff, *A Prologue to National Development Planning,* end note 3 (Greenwood Press, 1986).
7 Manzoor Ahmed and Philip H. Coombs, *Education for Rural Development: Case Studies for Planners* (prepared by World Bank and UNICEF, 1975).
8 Mahbul al Haq, *The Poverty Curtain.*

2 Present approaches for communication, learning and behaviour change

1 Dr Soedjatmoko, *Work in Progress* 9, 1 (Tokyo: UN University).
2 Robert S. McNamara, President of the World Bank, 1968–81; *Addresses of Robert S. McNamara 1968–1981* (Baltimore and London: Johns Hopkins University Press, 1981).
3 R. L. Lesher, 'The Voice of Business: A Vision for Education' (*Burrelle's,* 27 February 1992).
4 See assessments of T & V evaluations in I. S. MacDonald, 'Extension Methodology' – a paper for the International Extension Seminar, China (May 1992).
5 Produced quarterly by the Clearing House for Development Communication, funded by USAID. It was managed for fifteen years

by the Academy for Education Development and is now managed by the International Institute for Research, both in Washington DC.

6 Produced quarterly since 1978 by the UN Economic and Social Commission for Asia and the Pacific, Bangkok.

7 Lord Perry of Walton, founder of the Open University in the UK, Bernal Lecture: 'Science and Education', given at The Royal Society, London, 25 April 1989.

8 Peruvian Project on Primary Health Care. Pilot project implemented by PROMETHEUS PHC and financed by PRICOR Project of USAID.

9 B. M. Woods, *Choice and Management of Technology in Developing Countries* 11 (World Bank Projects Policy Department, 1986).

10 Joel Gomez and Leonel Valdivia, *Final Evaluation of National Rural Training Center and National Campesino Training Institute* (Washington DC: Creative Associates, 1985).

11 Lesotho Distance Teaching Centre, *A Cost Benefit Analysis of the LDTC's Assistance Fund* (Maseru, 1985); and J. Hoxeng, 'A Semi-systematic Approach to Nonformal Education', in Motilal Sharma (ed.) *Systems Approach: Its Applications in Education*, Bombay: Himalaya Publishing House, 1985).

3 Why?

1 T. Winograd and F. Flores, *Understanding Computers and Cognition: a New Foundation for Design* (Norwood, N.J.: Ablex Publishing Corporation, 1986).

2 See Professor Claude Ake's 'Sustaining Development on the Indigenous' in the Background Papers for *The Long-Term Perspective Study of Sub-Saharan Africa* (World Bank, 1990).

3 *The New Economics of Information*, by T. Stonier, N. Jayaweera and J. Robertson (1989), and the work cited in it reflect leading work by economists who are attempting to reposition the 'economic ladder' in order to take account of information and communication in development.

4 Robert S. McNamara, President of the World Bank, 1968–81; *Addresses of Robert S. McNamara 1968–1981* (Baltimore and London: Johns Hopkins University Press, 1981).

5 Andre Spier, background paper prepared for the first South African Informatics Consortium meeting (May 1992).

4 Digital technology systems for public use

1 Michael D. Dertouzos, Director, Laboratory for Computer Science, MIT.

2 N. Seshagiri, 'Informatics as a Tool for Development – A Long Term Perspective', Natural Informatics Centre, New Delhi, (1990).

3 *The Washington Post*, Business Sector, 19 January 1992.

4 Department of Defense Military Manpower Training Report FY 1992, April 1991.

5 *Training Magazine,* Survey, October 1991.
6 This section includes material from *Community Learning Network: a Mobilization Plan for the Implementation of a National Technology and Information Delivery System,* US Chamber of Commerce draft (December 1991).
7 US Chambers of Commerce, *Plans for AMERICA 2000 Program* (1991).
8 Gary J. Handler, Head of Network Planning at Bellcore (a large electronics corporation in the USA).
9 EPIE: Education Production Information Exchange Institute.

5   Implications and applications

1 John Sculley, Chairman and CEO, Apple Computers Inc., *Global Markets, Global Education* (1989).
2 Robert S. McNamara, President of the World Bank, 1968–81; *Addresses of Robert S. McNamara 1968–1981* (Baltimore and London: Johns Hopkins University Press, 1981).
3 Food Insecurity in Africa – 'The Challenge of Hunger in Africa Today', World Bank.
4 End note 13 *Our Common Future,* Report of UN World Commission on Environment and Development, headed by Gro Harlem Brundtland, Prime Minister of Norway (1988).

6   A new paradigm: a realm of new opportunity

1 John Sculley, Chairman and CEO, Apple Computers Inc., *Global Markets, Global Education* (1989).
2 Thomas Khun (ed. Fredrick Suppe), *The Structure of Scientific Theories* (Urbana: University of Illinois Press, 1974).
3 For this the author is indebted to John Carver in Johannesburg.
4 CGIAR: the Consultative Group on International Agricultural Research.

Index